Praise for *Those Who Wander*

"With riveting reporting and an abundance of compassion, Vivian Ho introduces us to a new genus of young wanderers. An important book for anyone interested in true American crime. Impossible to put down."

—Fox Butterfield, author of *In My Father's House*

"Written with honesty and elegance, *Those Who Wander* is also a work of masterful reporting. Vivian Ho is a determined, disciplined writer with a firm command of narrative and artful storytelling skills. This book is a page-turner that addresses the under-recognized but critical social problem of aimless young people whose search to find themselves can sometimes turn dangerous."

—Elizabeth Mehren, author of *Born Too Soon*

THOSE
WHO
WANDER

THOSE
WHO
WANDER

AMERICA'S LOST STREET KIDS

VIVIAN HO

Published by Little A, New York

www.apub.com

Amazon, the Amazon logo, and Little A are trademarks of Amazon.com, Inc., or its
affiliates.

ISBN-13: 9781503903739 (hardcover)
ISBN-10: 1503903737 (hardcover)
ISBN-13: 9781503903722 (paperback)
ISBN-10: 1503903729 (paperback)

Cover design by Faceout Studio, Tim Green

Printed in the United States of America

First edition

To those who wander: may you one day find
what you seek.
To my husband, Drew,
the compass that guides me home.

AUTHOR'S NOTE

This book does not claim to have the answers. This was a tough truth for me to accept, as I'd expect it to be for any journalist—finding answers is what we're supposed to do. But in the months I spent traveling around the country, talking to street kids, former street kids, housing advocates, trauma experts, social workers, and juvenile psychologists, I couldn't come up with one singular clear-cut solution for helping this population and ending youth homelessness.

Those who work with these kids will tell you it's simple—homeless people need housing. But I'd ask, How do we keep kids from homelessness in the first place? How do we stop them from experiencing the sort of hurt that drives them into the streets, where they will only experience more hurt, and, in turn, hurt others? How do we prevent tragedies such as the 2015 murders of Audrey Carey and Steve Carter from ever happening again?

I did not find an answer to those questions. I did not find an answer in the extensive talks I had with Morrison Haze Lampley, the convicted ringleader behind the killings, nor did I find one in the hundreds of hours of interviews I conducted over the course of my reporting. What I found, instead, were some incredible and fascinating human beings—human beings that so many of us pass every day on the streets without even a second glance. Human beings who, when they're not being overlooked, are considered nuisances, blights on our neighborhoods, or worse. Human beings, each of whom has their own unique and oftentimes heartbreaking story to tell—if only someone were to listen. If only we were to listen.

This book does not claim to solve homelessness. But in researching this issue, I learned to listen to these kids, to their stories and dreams and traumas and laughter. All we can hope now is that we hear what they have to say.

PROLOGUE

The Cabin in Oregon

Near the Oregon-Washington border lies a half acre of land, hidden amid the babbling brooks and lush greenery of the Pacific Northwest. The road leading to it winds up from Highway 30, growing narrower and narrower with each mile traveled up the mountain.

Past the multiple "No Trespassing" signs along the road, past the rushing creeks curving between the trees, a lengthy gravel driveway leads up to the property. The Clatskanie River bisects the land, clear and full and plentiful. The waterway has grown so much over the years that the far side almost abuts the back of the original cabin, which is held up and away from the water on log stilts. A rickety makeshift bridge, just big enough for a Harley-Davidson motorcycle to cross, provides dry passage to the other side of the property that ends at the bottom of a hill on which wild clover grows with abandon. Behind the cabin, two young sequoias, only decades old, stand tall near a large firepit made for family dinners and late nights of stargazing, relaxing, and wasting time in the company of those with whom time could never be considered wasted.

This was where Morrison Haze Lampley and his teenage paramour, Lila Scott Alligood, were heading in the fall of 2015. Before the bloodshed, before the violence, before the panicked drive to Portland,

Oregon, in a murdered man's car, there was a dream, and it all centered around this swath of land.

This land, according to Haze, has been in his family for at least one hundred years and is deeded to all the male descendants of the original owner. Therefore, the land is rightfully his, in a way, and so in September 2015, Haze and Lila packed up their meager belongings, hopped on their longboards, and headed north from San Diego.

"It was always in the back of my mind that I would end up at the cabin," Haze said. Within weeks of meeting Lila, he had told her about it, filling her head with the same dreams that danced in his. The deed supposedly includes mineral and water rights, and the plan was to get up there and start a marijuana farm. But more than that, Haze fantasized about doing it all, becoming a self-sustaining farmer and living off the land and the creek crawdads, never having to see another person again, outside of Lila, who he believed was the love of his life. At the cabin, they could finally escape. They could finally get off the streets and leave their lives of precarious uncertainty, freeing themselves from the violence and hunger and hard drugs that beckoned them from all directions. They could finally be in charge of their own destinies.

"We would have only come down for supplies," Haze said. "We'd sell a little pot to make ends meet. We'd never have to leave again."

It was a novel dream for someone who had spent most of his life both leaving and being left. Haze hadn't been to the property in years, but he could recall to the tiniest detail what it looks like, as if he had visited it every day in his mind's eye. The sequoias had been planted by his great-grandmother, when he and his younger brother were infants. Giant rocks enclose the firepit, except for a section where the family had laid a few bricks for grilling. The driveway can fit exactly three small RVs, and maybe two or three cars, and right off to the side of the driveway is the giant outhouse.

He couldn't say how many times he had gone there as a youth, but he remembered an uncle dangling him over the bridge so he could wash his hands in the creek. He remembered stepping on a nail somewhere on the property. A quick, sharp hurt that could be easily remedied—a world apart from the pain he experienced for almost all his life, living on the streets, dealing and using hard drugs, and getting abused everywhere he turned.

The cabin in Oregon served as a respite for him during his nomadic childhood, a place he knew would always exist even if he could not be there. It was the smallest piece of stability for a child who had no concept of the term, a place he could call his own when so much of what surrounded him did not belong to him.

And in his later years, it became his touchstone. His endgame. His haven from the madness that was his entire existence.

"It was mine, and nobody could take that away from me," he said, his eyes fierce. "The cabin, the dream—no matter what the world has taken from me, this was mine. This was mine, and nobody could take it."

The cabin in Oregon was where his story was supposed to end, but it was here that it truly began. He believed this land to be his birthright. What he inherited instead was generations of drug addiction, mental illness, and hurt that would go on to irrevocably shape the outcome of his life—and the lives of countless others.

ONE

San Rafael, California
April 2017

The victims' families were still crying quietly when Chief Deputy Public Defender David Brown stood to address the packed courtroom in Marin County, California. Next to him, his client, Morrison Haze Lampley, remained seated, his unruly mop of sandy-brown hair pulled back into a neat knot. Though the emotional and heartfelt statements from the victims' families had drawn tears from many in the gallery, as well as from his two codefendants, Lampley—who goes by Haze—kept his expressionless stare focused on the table in front of him, just as he had for the majority of the legal proceedings.

David Brown had worn a similar mask over the past year and a half, one of practiced stoicism shaped from years of courtroom experience. A gangly man with an almost constantly furrowed brow, he withstood with reluctance the onslaught of television cameras and microphones shoved in his face after each court appearance, declining the podium-pounding showboating that comes naturally to attorneys presented with high-profile cases. Even within the courtroom, he played the details close to his chest, refusing to feed the ravenous reporters that he tried to bar from the proceedings as they sought to make sense of two cold-blooded killings that had horrified the Bay Area.

But on the day Haze Lampley, his teenage girlfriend, and his long-time acquaintance were to be sentenced for the murders of twenty-three-year-old Audrey Carey and sixty-seven-year-old Steve Carter, Brown spoke to the court with the candor of an attorney who knew that his client was about to spend the rest of his life in prison. In the rushed bluntness he had become known for, Brown laid out the brutal reality of Haze's twenty-four years on this earth: the neglect, the homelessness, the abuse, the mental illness. He was "deprived of everything a child needs," Brown said, dosed with LSD as a toddler, shooting up drugs by the age of eleven. A psychiatrist once described him as a "feral child."

"Haze would have fared no worse or no better if he had been dropped off on a street corner after he was born," Brown said.

Then he turned to the front row of the gallery, where the victims' families sat.

"This is not offered as an excuse," Brown said to them, "but as an attempt to understand why we're all here."

～

What "here" meant differed for each person in the courtroom that day. In the simplest of terms, "here" was the end of an eighteen-month ordeal that began in October 2015 when three young drifters robbed and fatally shot Audrey Carey in the bushes of San Francisco's Golden Gate Park and then went on to kill Steve Carter for his car keys on a popular hiking trail in Marin County, just over the Golden Gate Bridge.

For the family members of Steve Carter, a respected tantra instructor who had moved back to California to support his wife through chemotherapy, and Audrey Carey, a free-spirited young girl with a bright future, "here" was a hell created by three monsters—Haze Lampley, his nineteen-year-old girlfriend, Lila Scott Alligood, and Sean Angold, their twenty-five-year-old friend—for whom no amount of prison time could make up for the lives they stole.

"It's not like those people just killed Steve," said Lokita Carter, Steve's widow. "They killed a huge chunk of me. They killed a whole other part of another human being."

In a statement read at the sentencing by a prosecutor, Audrey's mother, Isabelle Tremblay, denounced all three as "proof that evil exists." "You are not human beings," she wrote.

Her statement was an emotional, stinging barb, pulled from a deep place of grief to pierce into the hearts of the ones to whom it was directed. Lila sobbed through the reading, her attorney patting her on the back, while Sean kept his head down, his eyes damp. But months later, Haze shrugged at the vitriol directed at him and his two codefendants that day. "Unspeakable monsters," Isabelle Tremblay had called them. It wasn't the first time, Haze said, that he'd been called a monster.

It wasn't even the first time he had been called such as it pertained to this case. Throughout the proceedings, observers and those with knowledge of the case dismissed Haze as a "psychopath," an amoral creature sowing chaos everywhere he turned. They remarked on his "dead" eyes, his blank stare, the way he never reacted to anything in court.

Authorities were quick to paint him as the ringleader, the one who called the shots, the one who pulled the trigger in both the killings. In the realm of culpability, he had the most blood on his hands, they said, and that was reflected in the charges and sentencing. Sean was sentenced to fifteen years to life for the murder of solely Steve Carter, as part of the plea deal for his testimony. Lila was sentenced to fifty years to life, while Haze received a one-hundred-year sentence.

A "monster," they called him, but before his attorney's statement at the sentencing, few had stopped to consider what had made him this way. Few had stopped to consider what sort of life he had lived that had allowed him to deem it acceptable to rob two strangers at gunpoint, knowing full well that any misstep could end in bloodshed. Few had stopped to consider the sort of misfortunes that had shaped him into the type of young man who could witness up close the gore from one murder and still feel unaffected enough to pull the trigger on a second human being just days later. And even fewer had stopped to consider that the misfortunes that had made Haze who he is today are the same ones that have driven countless kids to a life of aimless homelessness—that the demons that haunt Haze, Lila, and Sean are the same that haunt the youth we pass on the streets every day, squatting along city sidewalks amid a cloud of body odor and marijuana smoke.

Because for Haze, Lila, and Sean, "here" was the abrupt end of a complicated and treacherous journey through their youth, one riddled with violence, drug use, terror, and crime. "Here" was the last stop of an unforgiving path on which millions of kids, teenagers, and young adults find themselves traveling each day, wandering across the country with little more than the packs on their back and nowhere to call home.

~

The tearful sentencing unfolded in the same courthouse that had been made famous by Angela Davis and the Black Panthers in the 1970s. Located in the heart of Marin County, the Civic Center is an architectural marvel designed by Frank Lloyd Wright shortly before his death, all chic curves and sleek glass atria. As the crime reporter for the *San Francisco Chronicle*, I had spent a chunk of the eighteen months it took to reach this point in the case crammed shoulder-to-shoulder with other local journalists in a modish wood-paneled court-room, scribbling down every gruesome, bloody detail of the killings under a bizarre spherical light fixture that reminded me of a cartoon spaceship. At times, being in that stylized courtroom felt like stepping into a topsy-turvy alternate reality—at the center of which sat Haze, Lila, and Sean. Eighteen months prior, deputies had marched them into the courtroom, all in their jail-issued striped jumpsuits and with their heads shaved—authorities had said they had bugs living in their tangled, matted hair when they arrived in Marin County. For a short time, their bald heads added another surreal layer to an already surreal situation. At their sentencing, eighteen months later, their short but clean locks, now long enough that they could pull back into buns, seemed to signify more than just the passage of time.

So few crimes happen in this affluent little county that are considered high-profile enough to tempt the San Francisco–based reporters into making the forty-minute drive over the Golden Gate Bridge, but each miniscule hearing and court appearance in this case had television satellite trucks lined up in the main parking lot. The media attention was so great that I had to make a conscious effort to arrive early to ensure I would even get into the courtroom—beyond the other reporters, every calendar item in this case brought in scores of court gadflies, lookie-loos, and various other forms of concerned citizenry.

We at the *Chronicle* began referring to Haze, Lila, and Sean as "the drifters" pretty much from the start, and the term caught on with other news outlets as well. We'd slug our stories in the daily budgets with it and drop the label in casual conversation—it got to the point where I'd cancel plans with my friends because of "the drifters," and they'd fully understand what I meant. Thinking back, I'm not sure why "drifters" became the term that stuck, but we cycled through a number of other descriptions for the three—"young transients," I wrote in September 2016. The "accused murder trio," said the *San Francisco Examiner* in October 2015. "Three young itinerants," according to the *Marin Independent Journal* in November 2015; and "murderous vagabonds" in April 2017, for the sentencing. "Lost souls" was what Marin County sheriff's spokesperson Lieutenant Doug Pittman called them at the press conference announcing their arrests, an oddly poetic phrase from someone in law enforcement, and we all ran that quote for about a week before tiring of it.

All the media coverage made a point to reference their youth—at the time of their arrest in October 2015, Lila had just turned eighteen, while Haze and Sean were twenty-three and twenty-four, respectively. At twenty-six, I was just a few years older than they were when this all began, yet as I sat there in that courtroom, eighteen months later, I felt as if there were decades between us. The defendants' youth contributed to the media frenzy around the trial, but that was just one of several elements of this case that captured the attention of the Bay Area. There was a senselessness to these crimes that nobody could comprehend, a disruption to the regularly scheduled programming of our prescribed acceptable behavior in society. The fact that the three killed two strangers was especially chilling—according to the Federal Bureau of Investigation's Uniform Crime Reporting Program, only about 10 percent of all homicides nationwide involve strangers—and the fact that they committed these murders within days of each other led many to wonder whether there had been, or could have been, more had the police not arrested them when they did.

But most of all, what terrified Bay Area residents was the fact that Haze, Lila, and Sean could have been any one of the hundreds of kids, teens, and young adults we pass on the streets every day. The transient youth population is especially vibrant in California, to the point that they have their own categorization within the realm of homelessness—street kids. Mention the term "street kid" to anyone on the West Coast and they will know exactly of whom you speak—the tough and, at times, confrontational kids with dreadlocked hair who spend all day lounging around in the parks or on the sidewalks. Yes, they're homeless, but somehow they're different from the downtrodden folks who line up with carts outside of soup kitchens. They have neither money nor steady employment, but they're not destitute. They're not all kids in the sense that they're under the age of eighteen, yet they all somehow have both a youthfulness and an aged presence about them.

These kids were the backbone of the vagabond counterculture that became a part of San Francisco's identity, but following the slayings of Audrey Carey and Steve Carter, they became scapegoats for law-abiding citizens to fear the most. Complaints that supposedly progressive Bay Area residents had never felt acceptable to voice before spilled over in a frenzied witch hunt, as they struggled to make peace with the dichotomy of their free-spirited history that accepted and celebrated these wanderers, and their current, unpredictable reality of street kids setting up tents anywhere they pleased, using hard drugs, urinating wherever, and holding loud all-night parties outside people's homes. At best, these kids blocked sidewalks and lived on handouts. At worst, they were a violent, threatening presence who fought among themselves and scared away customers from local businesses.

For these Bay Area residents, "here" was the possibility that these kids who had long been part of the fabric of San Francisco life now had the potential to be the monsters, to be the evil, that tore through Audrey Carey's and Steve Carter's families. "Here" was the chance that you or someone you love could be the next Audrey or Steve.

~

No one knows for certain how many homeless youth are out there right now, with policymakers on the federal and local levels at odds over what exactly constitutes homelessness—and at what age someone emotionally and psychologically stunted from living on the streets can no longer be considered a youth. Even some who fall within the broadest parameters of homelessness reject the loaded term because, while claiming one's homelessness grants access to opportunities when it comes to housing, health care, and funding, it still carries a significant stigma and helplessness that many are unwilling to accept. Researchers at the University of Chicago's Chapin Hall attempted to count the country's homeless youth in 2017, and found that one in ten young adults ages eighteen to twenty-five had experienced some form of homelessness for a period of twelve months or more. Half of those individuals admitted outright to experiencing explicit homelessness, while the other half claimed to be couch surfing and surviving off the mercy of others. That same study found that one in thirty youth ages thirteen to seventeen had been homeless for at least a twelve-month period, with three-quarters of those individuals admitting to explicit homelessness, whether because they ran away or were kicked out of their homes, and the remaining quarter reporting that they, like their young-adult counterparts, survived by staying with acquaintances, hopping from couch to couch.

That all boils down to an estimated 3.5 million young adults and 700,000 youth who have experienced prolonged homelessness at some point in their lives. And each one of those lives contains an unknown history of trauma and pain, be it what drove them to the streets or what they found waiting for them when they got there—emotional baggage that will drive a good number of them to a life of hard drugs and mental instability, until, bit by bit, they fade from the burgeoning human beings they once were into just another statistic to rattle off in a book.

Even before the killings, street kids were regarded, in San Francisco and beyond, with a level of disdain reserved specifically for this particular subset of the homeless population—and this disdain has only continued. What little compassion we have for the homeless is saved for those who fit our ideal version of homelessness: those down on their luck, struggling to make their way off the street. Those who want to better themselves and their circumstances, but who must overcome certain obstacles to do so. On the flip side, there are the street kids. The vagabonds. The drifters. The free spirits, taking advantage of our goodwill to neglect the responsibilities set by a social contract by which we all must abide. A common narrative pushed about these kids is that they are homeless by choice. They could easily not be homeless, so the narrative goes, if they would just get a job. If they would stop being lazy. If only they didn't want this free-living life. These kids are a middle finger to the American myth of resilience and perseverance, in which anyone can succeed if they pull themselves up by their bootstraps. These kids just refuse to try, their critics say. They refuse to live by the societal contract to which we all adhere.

To street kids and those who work with them, this narrative is not only inaccurate, but also damaging. Because for the majority of these kids, the choice is between homelessness and, for example, "Do I want to stay at home and get raped every night by my uncle?" in the words of Christian Garmisa-Calinsky, who ran a nonprofit that found housing for street kids in San Francisco. "Or like it was for me: Do I want to stay home and get my bones continually broken by my mother?"

I had met Christian just days after the three were arrested in Portland, Oregon, at a heated Haight Street community meeting in which he acted as the voice of reason, reminding the angry masses that it'd be unfair to paint all street kids with the same brush and assume all have the potential for murder. After all, just a decade ago, Christian had been part of this population, sleeping in parks with his pack underneath him and his legs tangled over his bicycle to prevent theft. Like Haze, he too was described as "feral," having been homeless on and off since the age of twelve. "The only life I knew was packing all my stuff into my pack and being able to leave really quick," he said.

In his time on the streets and in the work he does now, he's come across countless kids with the same sort of background as Haze, Lila, and Sean. They run away to escape a life in which it was beaten into them that they were nothing, less than nothing, and then they are taken in by the streets, where the last of their humanity is ripped from them. Because on the streets, there is no black and white. There is no good and evil. There is only survival.

You can't pull yourself up by your bootstraps if you have no boots. You can't persevere if the trauma you suffered as a child makes it impossible for you to look a person in the eye, if the only way of life you know is a needle in your arm to numb the pain.

~

"This is not offered as an excuse, but as an attempt to understand why we're all here." I had been having conversations with Christian about this very point for weeks before David Brown made this statement in court. Christian had needled me for wondering about what forced these kids into the streets, into a life of violence, drug abuse, instability, and—in the case of Haze, Lila, and Sean—murder. "You should focus on the solution, on how to get them off the streets," he said. Because for those who work with this population, they already know all too well that "here" is what happens when our children are failed, time and time again, by the systems in place. "Here" is the end result of instability, neglect, abuse, drug addiction, mental illness, and violence that is only perpetuated with the more time these hurt kids are forced to live as homeless transients, in a community of other hurt kids just as unpredictable and in need of help as they are. "Here" began for generations of youth before Haze, Lila, or Sean were even born.

The circumstances of Haze's life that led him to "here" are far more complicated, conflicting, and crushing than what his attorney laid out in court the day of his sentencing. They are circumstances similar to those suffered by Sean and Lila, similar to those suffered by the millions that remain on the streets each night while these three wait out their prison sentences.

This means little to the families of Audrey Carey and Steve Carter. They have had to endure an unspeakable loss because of these circumstances—circumstances beyond their control—a loss for which there is no excuse. But these circumstances are not being offered as an excuse. They are being offered as a way to understand this generation of lost youth, a generation of hurt kids just like Haze, Lila, and Sean, many of whom find themselves every day teetering at the same precipice of no return where those three stood in October 2015. "Here" is not Americana folklore, Jack Kerouac, and the Summer of Love coming home to roost. "Here" is a crisis, decades in the making. "Here" is millions of hurt kids, abandoned on the streets, knowing little more than doing whatever it takes to survive.

We were "here" before Audrey Carey and Steve Carter were mercilessly gunned down, before they even crossed paths with the three who would kill them. We were "here" before Haze Lampley took his first snort of heroin, before Lila Alligood smoked her first hit of meth, before Sean Angold's doomed chance encounter with the couple in San Francisco.

The question, now, is where we go from "here."

TWO

B uena Vista Park sits at the center of Haight Street, a hilly enclave of brush and trees in the birthplace of the Summer of Love. Downhill from the park, Haight is just another San Francisco street, with a mix of dive and hipster bars, overpriced eateries, new trendy apartment complexes, and beautiful old Victorians packed with roommates making the most out of the last remaining rent-controlled apartments in a city with a skyrocketing cost of living. But head west from Buena Vista Park, and Haight Street will show its roots. The storefronts display tie-dye and psychedelic lettering, and the bright street art splashed upon the walls and sidewalks pays homage to the Grateful Dead, the band that made it all happen out of their Ashbury Street home in the 1960s. Much has changed in this neighborhood over the past six decades— just as an example, a restaurant run by a burlesque performer named Magnolia Thunderpussy that specialized in erotic-themed desserts is now a microbrewery called Magnolia Brewing that caters to the sort of clean-cut crowd that Haight regulars would once have decried as yuppies. Yet a piece of the '60s remains frozen in time on Haight, in the street kids gathered along this stretch, panhandling for cash, sucking down cigarettes, and strumming on beat-up guitars and ukuleles.

These kids might have better-quality camping gear and might use their cracked-screen iPhones to sneak onto nearby cafés' Wi-Fi networks and scroll through funny memes, but to the tourists trundling by in their double-decker buses, these kids could be the same unwashed youth with oversize packs and mangy dogs that flocked here when Janis Joplin roamed the street. The tourists can still get that Summer of Love experience when they drop some coins into the hat of some kid with a creative sign asking for money for weed or beer, or hand off their leftovers to a group lounging outside Coffee to the People at the corner of Masonic Avenue.

Buena Vista Park is a favorite hangout for these kids, a group of whom can be found, on any given day, lying out on the flat lawn outside the park's Haight Street entrances. Dog owners and joggers frequent this park, but the privacy and isolation created by the thick vegetation and arduous climbs make Buena Vista a prime spot for less healthy exploits. It's a park of steep inclines—to get into the heart of it, you have to climb a set of steps, and from there it's burning calves and an uptick in pulse until you reach the top. Before the days of Grindr and the more mainstream acceptance of the LGBTQ community, gay men came here for random hookups and romantic rendezvous. Heavy drug users call the park "Tweaker Hill," and hide out in the brush when they need to shoot up. And for the transient youth still drawn to the Haight for its history of love, peace, and acceptance, Buena Vista Park is the perfect place to spend the night.

It was here that I was introduced to the world of street kids, through my first assignment for the *San Francisco Chronicle*. I started at the *Chronicle* in 2011 as a summer intern, and ended up staying for almost seven years, moving through the newsroom as a breaking-news reporter before taking on the crime and criminal-justice beat. My editor in the summer of 2011 had a sick sense of humor and thought it'd be funny to throw the intern a particularly gruesome story—the case of a man who was found half-naked and partially burned in Buena

Vista Park. The man's death ended up being a hookup gone awry and had nothing to do with the street kids, but most of the neighbors' first thoughts were that "it was probably a homeless person." Their guess wasn't without foundation—less than a year before, a homeless man had stabbed to death another homeless man in the park in a dispute over a woman—but I found it fascinating that the supposedly progressive and accepting neighbors would write off the street kids, calling them an innocuous bunch who kept to themselves, and yet look in their direction whenever violence occurred in the vicinity. I quoted one neighbor in the story who speculated that the murderer was probably a street kid, and then later, among the garbage heap of online comments, someone purporting to be that neighbor expressed anger that I didn't include the second half of his quote, where he had said he found the street kids to be "mostly harmless."

But that's San Francisco. It's a city of nuances and contradictions, where residents want to have it both ways without realizing the impossibility of such. It's a city where innovation and growth come at the expense of the artists and poets who built its reputation of free thinking and progress. It's a city that welcomes all walks of life, yet bears graffiti deriding "techie scum." It's a city of extreme disparities, where young, hoodie-wearing engineers with their faces glued to the latest and most expensive smartphones can walk by homeless encampments where the level of indigence has elicited comparisons to the slums of Mumbai and Calcutta.

It's a city I arrived in with the intention of staying for just three months and instead made my home for almost the entirety of my twenties. It's a city that will dazzle you with its quirks and its beauty, with its indefatigable ability to make you fall in love, again and again and again. It's a city that will inevitably break your heart, when, over time, you begin to see the cracks and blemishes so carefully veiled by its foggy charms. I arrived here believing there was no place like home, no place like New England for a wicked pissah Masshole like me, only to learn that there was no place like San Francisco—yes, a city of nuances and contradictions, a city whose residents keep fighting for the impossible because if there were ever a place for the impossible to become possible, it'd be San Francisco.

Like most dumb twenty-two-year-olds fresh out of college, I thought I knew more than I actually did that summer. I read a couple of Joan Didion essays, bought some sunscreen, and felt sufficiently prepared for California. I expected hippies and weirdos and protests and patchouli oil—and, of course, homelessness. "There'll be a level of homelessness unlike anything you've seen on the East Coast," people warned me. "It's because of the better weather," a friend explained. "It's because San Francisco is more lenient toward the homeless," another person told me, "because of its history with hippies and free love and acceptance and whatnot." And, with my first assignment for the *Chronicle*, I wrongly inferred that many of this population chose to be homeless. A member of the neighborhood association whom I interviewed for the story told me there were two populations: the standard homeless—the majority of whom suffer from mental disorders or substance abuse issues—and then the street kids. One of my *Chronicle* colleagues described the two groups as the "homeless" and the "hard-core homeless," with the homeless-by-choice street kids falling into the former.

It was under this preconceived notion that I met Dave. Eager to impress on my first assignment, I told my editor that I wanted to head into the park at night, when the street kids would be bunking down and therefore easier to find. "No parks after dark," he grumbled—another strange San Francisco concept, created in part because of the large homeless population who sleeps in the parks at night. Schoolchildren grow up adhering to this adage, understanding that the lovely out-door spaces where they play during the day become dangerous at night because of the homeless.

I decided to try the park "before light," and headed over just as the sun began to peek through the thick trees, when everything was quiet in that beautiful predawn way. The birds were just starting to wake, though the city had not, and the air felt cool and refreshing through my light blazer. Like so many of San Francisco's lush outdoor spaces, Buena Vista Park has a way of transporting you out of the urban milieu. Once you're inside the park, the shade of tall trees and the smell of damp dirt can make you forget that you're in a city. That morning, I passed just one lone dog walker, and for a few minutes, I felt like I had this entire secret forest on a hill to myself.

I kept to the main paved path, my sweat-slick feet slipping around in my sensible flats with each step I took farther up the hill. I was just starting to worry that I wouldn't find any of those dreaded street kids when I heard a rustling coming from the bushes. And there was Dave. "Good morning," he greeted me, as if we were just two neighbors passing by one another on our way to grab a coffee before work.

In the article, I described him as dragging with him "a dusty black sleeping bag, a backpack, and the scent of last night's cigarettes and this morning's hangover." He had a slight, wiry frame, not much taller than mine of five feet five; his dirty, chin-length brown hair hung in clumps around his thin face. He had a lip ring, some neck tattoos, and a small tattoo next to his eye. He wore a brown plaid shirt and tan overalls with a large rip in the back, and he had a bandanna tied around his neck that he referred to as his "skank." And for somebody who had just awakened, Dave Thompson, then twenty-four, was surprisingly chipper and more than willing to chat about his current existence.

I told him about the murder, and the neighbors' suspicions, which he quickly scoffed off. Street kids would never go so far as to murder— unless a rape was involved, and then "murder is totally called for," he said. "Nothing ever goes that far," he insisted. "There are some wing nuts out there, but not the street kids."

Dave didn't think of himself as homeless—he was "houseless," a global citizen who had been "everywhere." He grew up in the Detroit area and had been living on and off the streets since he was thirteen.

And he loved it. He was free. He woke up whenever he wanted, he did whatever he felt like doing. He got to travel—he was on his way to the annual Rainbow Family Gathering in Washington that year—and he had a dog, named Chicken, who was staying with some friends sleeping in Golden Gate Park. "Bad stuff happens to us," he told me, "but more good stuff happens." When you don't have to answer to anyone, life is one big party. When you have nowhere you belong, you are free.

~

Transients like Dave—and Haze, Lila, and Sean—go by a variety of different names: street kids, dirty kids, travelers, hippies, gutter punks, rail riders. Others call them *vagrants*, *drifters*, *hoboes* (though *hobo* is specifically reserved for the homeless who hop on trains). Some are just passing through, while others said they were just passing through months before and still remain. Some have a form of shelter, sleeping in beat-up cars and vans that barely run, while others sleep outdoors, in tents if they can get one, and out in the open if they cannot.

As the Chapin Hall study researchers found in conducting their count of homeless youth, the definition of this population varies according to whom you ask—and that includes Congress and the federal agencies in charge of allocating resources.

"One of the things we hear on a regular basis is that the [US Department of Health and Human Services] definition for emergency shelters is for youth up to the age of eighteen and the definition for emergency shelters funded by the [US Department of Housing and Urban Development] is for people eighteen and over," said Bryan Samuels, executive director of Chapin Hall at the University of Chicago. "If you're seventeen years old and in an emergency shelter and you turn eighteen, you would in theory have to leave one shelter and go to an adult shelter. But are eighteen-year-olds really adults? Should they really be served in an adult shelter? Or should the question be, Are you really an adult at twenty-one? At what age do you become an adult? Or, if you're trying to get help for youth who are eighteen or nineteen years old, are they more willing to use it if there are youth their own age, rather than at a shelter with adults in their forties?"

. Talking to this population, I found that their definition of what makes a kid and a youth varies as well. By society's standards, at eighteen you are legally an adult, but ask any eighteen-year-old whether they feel that way and most will say no. The streets, and living without a set home, further complicate that. The streets, and the company you keep while living on them, are a twisted sort of neverland. Not only do you never grow up because your development is stunted, but you also spend your whole life thinking of yourself as a kid, hanging out with other kids and shirking society's concepts of adulthood and responsibility—and you grow up way too fast because you have to, in order to survive. This population is stuck in a maturation limbo that is both of their own making and completely beyond their control. Some advocates who work with homeless youth have individuals as old as thirty-five in their programs.

No one has a clear idea of how many of these kids are the traveling type. The travelers tend to blend in with the ones who remain where they are, and together they while away their days panhandling—or "spanging"—for cash, smoking pot, hanging out with their friends, figuring out where to get their next meal, and planning where they'll spend the night. It takes a certain amount of wherewithal and savvy to travel while homeless, and not every kid is at a place mentally or emotionally to do so. Michael Niman, a journalism professor at Buffalo State College who spent time studying this community, said he found that homeless travelers tended to be overwhelmingly white. "To travel as a vagrant is white privilege," he said. The Chapin Hall study, on the other hand, found that African American youth had an 83 percent increased risk of having experienced homelessness, meaning there is some level of disconnect within this population.

Homeless youth also differ from city to city. In New York, the majority of homeless youth are "young people who were born and raised in the five boroughs," said Jamie Powlovich, executive director of the Coalition for Homeless Youth in New York. "Drifters, street youth— that's not what we have here." In New York, there's less of a celebration of street kid culture than on the West Coast, where homeless youth almost take pride in their status and allow themselves to be visibly vagrant. In New York, homeless kids try to conceal their unstable living arrangements, but that doesn't make them any less homeless. "They are couch surfing, they are exchanging sex for shelter, but they don't have anywhere else to go," Powlovich said.

There's no easy way to differentiate between who is traveling and who is not, beyond asking each individual we pass on the street. And even then the answer isn't always clear. Some may be traveling, some may be "thinking about it," some may have traveled at one point but are now settling down in one city, and some may be doing any variety or combination of the above. One formerly homeless woman I spoke with put it bluntly: When you travel, you have something to do. You have a hobby. Otherwise, you're just homeless.

In trying to understand the world from which Haze Lampley, Lila Alligood, and Sean Angold emerged, I've come to think of a street kid as any unaccompanied homeless individual up to the age of thirty. While many homeless youth employ a level of cunning and can find themselves a place to stay every so often, I think of street kids as the more visibly homeless, who spend most of their day on the streets or in the parks. Some do end up finding a way to spend some of their nights indoors, but others set up camp near their hangouts, making sure to break down their tents before the police come by to hassle them. Some street kids travel, hitchhiking where they need to go or spanging for just enough for a cheap Greyhound ticket. Some do not.

The ones who travel know through word of mouth which cities have the best resources for the homeless and which have the strongest street kid communities to lean on—on the East Coast, there's Asheville, North Carolina, and out west there's Eugene, Oregon; San Diego; Denver; and, of course, San Francisco. And in spite of recent efforts pushing to clear encampments and criminalize sitting or lying down on sidewalks, for the kids who wander around the country with no tether to hold them to one place, there is some truth in San Francisco's broad stereotypes. Its hippie history of welcoming those with unconventional lifestyles still draws many to its cool, fog-obscured hills. For the many youth identifying as part of the LGBTQ community—the Chapin Hall study found that LGBTQ youth had a 120 percent greater risk of experiencing homelessness than their heterosexual and cisgender counterparts—the city's record of advocating for LGBTQ rights and flying rainbow flags appeals to their quest for acceptance. Combined with the city's mild weather and abundance of open park spaces, San Francisco, a city with one of the highest costs of living in the country, has everything necessary for this population to survive.

Just forty-seven square miles large, San Francisco is a small enough city to cover on foot, despite its treacherous hills known for causing vertigo and for popping the clutches on manual transmissions. While Haight Street has the history, the homeless youth who settle in San Francisco have their pick of locations to set up camp. At Fisherman's Wharf, they can work the tourists for spare change, and in the Castro, LGBTQ youth can find the community they seek and access LGBTQ-specific services. The Tenderloin boasts a number of food kitchens and services for the homeless, as well as an almost blatantly open-air market for illegal hard drugs, while the Mission, which houses two of the city's homeless navigation centers, is close enough to the industrial nooks of the freeway overpasses that provide easy shelter for homeless encampments.

That morning in Buena Vista Park, Dave told me he was just passing through San Francisco. The last time he'd visited, he'd been sixteen. I brought up the concept of "homeless by choice," and Dave readily copped to this categorization. This was the life he chose. This was a life in which he could live free, going wherever he wanted whenever he felt like it. A small piece of me envied his freedom, his audacity to live a life considered unacceptable by society's rigid standards. But he never went into how or why he became homeless at the young age of thirteen—or whether it had been his choice then. He never told me how it was that he could wake up whenever he wanted when he clearly had to leave before the cops came by. And he never discussed the parts of his existence that led to his earlobe being torn and flapping next to his face like a limp flag of flesh, or to the scar he bore on his right cheek from a homeless man taking a scalpel to him one night.

"Of course they're going to say it's their choice," said Christian Garmisa-Calinsky, the former street kid who founded Taking it to the Streets, a nonprofit that connected homeless kids to housing and services. "Because what's the alternative? 'My life is crap'?"

Those who work with the homeless in San Francisco have long balked at the double standard placed on this population. By categorizing homelessness as a choice for some, we declare them less worthy of our sympathy, already worn thin to the point of nonexistence when it comes to the indigent. We ignore how few choices they had that made them choose a life on the streets, and we place an impossible expectation upon them: if you chose to be homeless, then you can also choose to not be.

"There's a common belief that all homeless people are lazy and they should go get a job, but that's almost impossible after you've slept outside a couple days," Christian said. "For a lot of these kids, it's like gas on a fire. Some of the kids are addicted to drugs, some of them have mental health issues. All of them have trauma. And then you have to worry about people stealing your stuff, you have to worry about being raped, you have to worry about being kidnapped, about being beat up, about your dog getting in a fight or taken, about the police messing you up. You start having grown folks messing with you every day and you start becoming even more agitated by authority, and then you don't want that anymore."

The more we reject them, Christian said, the more they reject us and their options become all the more sparse. I've spoken to dozens of street kids throughout the years. While some told me that they wanted out, off the streets and into a home, many more said that they enjoyed the life they had, wandering from place to place with no guarantee of shelter, food, or money. But they also saw life in absolutes, divided by just two choices: either they could be "free" and living on the streets, or they could be trapped in a cubicle and become one of the miserable, unhappy people who make their lives hell every day.

That sunny morning at Buena Vista Park, my introduction to the world of street kids lasted all of about twenty minutes. Dave chatted cheerfully as we made our way down the hill. He explained how street kids take care of their own and police their own, kicking out those who cause trouble and looking out for the ones who need it. And while violence was a fact of life for them, they'd never resort to murder. He told me he usually kept a knife on him for protection and tried to "stay in numbers" for safety.

We paused for him to gulp down some water at a fountain in the park before going down the steps to Haight Street. Dave was heading to Golden Gate Park to meet up with the friends who had taken care of his dog that night, and I—one of the zombies trapped in a cubicle that kids like Dave derided—had to go into work. I asked him for his last name, and he balked at first. "Nobody even knows my last name," he said, before giving it to me anyway. He flipped me off in the photo I took of him as proof of his existence, but gave me a hug before we parted ways.

I look back on my scant notes from that encounter, and my inexperience is apparent in the messy scrawl. I wish I had asked him more. I wish I had asked him why—why he continued living this precarious lifestyle in which his safety and well-being depended solely on the generosity and goodwill of others; why he did not want to leave a life where another homeless man could take a scalpel to his face, where in some instances "Murder is totally called for." I wish I had asked him whether he thought he could actually leave this life if he wanted to. Because with little to no guidance going into the streets, once they get there and experience what they believe to be freedom for the first time in their lives, it is hard to leave without adult intervention.

"I look at it this way: there's this road here, and this is the road that you're on when you first become homeless," Christian said. "It's all fun and games and you're smoking weed and doing whatever you're doing out here, and then you come to this crossroads. Over here, it's all bright with neon signs and it's really pretty. It's party time. You want to go down that one, but the dark road is adulting. No one was standing at that crossroads to say, 'Hey, Christian. That brightly lit road? It's fucked up. It might be bright and you might be able to see where you're going, but there's a train coming at you this way. The dark road is the one you're supposed to take.'"

Dave Thompson was the first street kid I ever met, but he would not be the last. You can't report on crime in San Francisco without coming in contact with this population, and the stories were endless. I spent time with them while covering the Occupy protests that sprouted up in major cities across the country, waiting out the long nights for the police raids to clear out the encampments. I wrote about the city's efforts to prevent them from loitering in public spaces, efforts that have done little but to criminalize their presence. I reported on transient kids arrested for assaults, carjackings, and yes, murder. In the eyes of the street kid community, the ones accused of those crimes were always the outliers. They were the tweakers, the druggies, the "scum." The article I wrote that seemed to capture the street kid spirit best involved a group of kids harassing and trying to oust a costumed street performer at Fisherman's Wharf who had earned a reputation as "Bad Elmo" in different cities around the country for yelling obscenities at tourists and running a pornography website called Welcome to Rape Camp. Although he was never convicted of crimes against children, the street kids viewed him as a child molester, and the only way to deal with a child molester was through "street justice." "It's up to the street kids to take care of the things the police can't," one kid told me proudly.

With each kid I interviewed, somewhere in the back of my mind, I'd think of Dave. I'd wonder whether he ever made it to the Rainbow Family Gathering like he had intended, or whether he was still somewhere out there, wandering and living free with his beagle-collie mix, Chicken. I didn't realize until much later how much he had influenced my perspective of this population. My reporting on street kids for years after my fateful meeting with Dave had been colored in the dusty earth tones of the garb he'd worn the day I met him, tinged in the scent of stale cigarette smoke and body odor.

In a lot of ways, meeting Dave influenced my reporting for the better. I came to San Francisco with almost six years of journalism under my belt—I had been interning out of professional newsrooms since I was seventeen—but the types of stories and people I had been exposed to up until then had existed very much within the same privileged, middle-class bubble in which I lived and was brought up. Within days of starting my first nine-to-five job out of college, I was thrown into a world that orbited in a completely different solar system than mine. I remember recoiling for just a beat when Dave went in for a hug. I had dressed for work that morning, wearing a lovely sky-blue ruffled top from Banana Republic that was made with that smooth silky material that all professional tops seem to be made of. Before I'd left for San Francisco, my mother and sister had delighted in building my new wardrobe of stiff and smart "casual professional" attire that I never felt comfortable wearing. *Is this dry-clean only?* I wondered as Dave leaned in, his arms open. *Am I going to have to dry-clean this?* I made a note to call my mom and ask. Yet, it was fine. Sure, Dave was a little smellier and dirtier than most of the people I'd interviewed and interacted with in the past. But I had genuinely enjoyed our conversation. I appreciated his candor and his willingness to share his life with me. Upon meeting Dave, I stopped thinking of these kids as some far-off concept and instead began seeing them as real people and real individuals with real stories to tell. Looking back, I'm ashamed that my first thought in that moment was my stupid top, but I can say that the hug I shared with Dave that day was the last time I took dry-cleaning into consideration when it came to human beings.

When I met Dave, I was twenty-two, two years younger than he was at the time. I was younger than Haze and Sean were, and only four years older than Lila was, when they killed Audrey Carey and Steve Carter. I was technically an adult, working an office job, wearing professional clothing, and paying rent, but my view of the world was still that of a sheltered child. There was good and there was bad, an order and a plan for everything. Everyone fit in their correct, neat little boxes. In meeting Dave, I accepted his sunny perspective on the lives of street kids and I applied it to all street kids. He only showed me the good, so I never considered the bad that they faced. I never considered that they could do bad things beyond the petty victimless acts they had to do to survive or to uphold the order within their community. With Dave as my window into this world, I saw these kids as just another part of the fabric that made San Francisco the quirky and fascinating Oz I grew to love and adopt as my home, as much a part of the city as the activists who rallied in front of City Hall and the nudists who strolled through the Castro. It was just as the Buena Vista Park neighbors had described: street kids were a "mostly harmless" bunch.

Until they weren't.

THREE

When I met Dave, I was nearing the end of a path that I had been raised to follow my entire life. Go to school. Get good grades. Go to college. Graduate. Get a job. Make money. The next stop on this path was not well defined. Get married, buy a house, start a family, yes—but then what? In the first two decades of our lives, we are socialized to reach certain milestones at a rapid pace, and then we are left with the rest of our lives stretching long and ominously ahead of us. We stay in our neat little boxes, and then we are sent down our respective conveyor belts, chugging toward some destination we can't ever see. What surprised me when I spoke with Dave was how appealing I found the life he described—how appealing it was to think of shaking off the shackles of what I was expected to do, of being able to forge my own path in the world, in a way not approved by the society that had ordered me onto my current trajectory.

I had laughed at my initial reaction. I wouldn't consider myself a squeamish or high-maintenance person, but I am used to certain comforts in life. I enjoy showering every day, answering nature's call in the privacy of an actual restroom, having clean sheets to sleep on at night. I get fussy when I'm hungry and cranky without a good night's sleep. I wouldn't make it more than a day in Dave's world.

Looking back, though, I can understand why the houseless life intrigued me. What gets lost far too often in the conversation about homeless youth is that, at the heart of it, the majority of these kids are just that: kids. Look past their baggage and the traumas that shaped them, past any mental illness or drug use, past their bravado and in-your-face swagger, and these kids aren't any different from the millions of others throughout this country who are worrying about their college essays, crying over inconsequential slights from their supposed friends, struggling with their appearance, and rebelling against the authority figures in their lives.

"When you're in your youth, you're trying to expand to fill yourself out, and they're trying to stick you in this little teeny tiny bottle and keep you there," said Sleepy, a thirty-seven-year-old traveling dirty kid I met on the road in Arizona. "That's probably the biggest factor that attracts everyone to this life. We've all felt that kind of oppression and this is a way to be away from that."

On top of the basic fight for survival and making do without the safety of a home, these kids are just trying to find their place in this world, a world that has told them time and time again that they are not welcome. When Reverend Larry Beggs founded Huckleberry House for Runaways in response to the growing underage runaway population flocking to San Francisco in the 1960s, he realized well before most that when kids ran, it was not just what they were running from, but what they were running to. These "lost children with windy feet," as one of the kids once described herself to him, were just searching for something better, searching for somewhere to belong.

More than fifty years later, this still rings true for the transient youth who continue to roam through the streets of San Francisco. Their actions may seem reckless, their decision-making rash, but therein lies the folly—and hubris—of youth. Just like your hometown teenagers trying beer for the first time, like the youth who toilet-paper and egg their neighbors' homes on Halloween, they go forth believing they are invincible, that they are beyond consequences, that nothing can get in their way.

For all the suffering they endured to drive them to the streets, and for all the further misery they experience once they get there, so many still carry with them a fragile innocence behind their hardened and dirty exteriors. Sometimes all the money they get comes from the kindness of strangers, so as hurt as they are or have been in the past, they haven't given up yet on believing in goodness, in a better life. They want more but do not yet know what that means. And so they search, leaving all they know in order to not just find their purpose, but understand it. They search, just like every other young person in the history of mankind. They search, just as twenty-three-year-old Audrey Carey was searching, when, on a whim, she bought a plane ticket to San Francisco one month before her murder. *"Et peu importe la destination, c'est le voyage qui compte,"* she told her mother, according to *La Presse*.

"Whatever the destination, it's the journey that counts."

∼

Audrey Carey arrived in San Francisco in September 2015 with a backpack full of camping gear and $600 in cash.

At twenty-three years old, the dreamy-eyed Quebecois traveler was embarking on her first solo trip, searching, like so many others her age, for not just adventure, but herself. Her mother, Isabelle Tremblay, told local Quebecois media that Audrey had recently dropped out of the University of Sherbrooke after realizing she didn't want to spend the rest of her life as a lawyer. "Do you not think that it's a little stupid that the world asks what we do in life?" Audrey asked her mother, according to *La Presse*. "Ask me what I am!" Following a hard summer planting trees in Abitibi, surprising and arduous work for a girl who grew up comfortably in a small city outside of Montreal, Audrey had declared, "I do not want to work between four walls." But what that meant, she did not know, and she soon found herself on her way to San Francisco.

It must have been both a relief and a thrill for the kindhearted girl to meet so many youth in San Francisco going through that same sort of soul-searching as she was. The city's history as a beacon for the counterculture meant that, fifty years after the Summer of Love, its streets and leafy parks still served as a hub for the homeless, the houseless, the drifters, and the restless. She emailed her mother on September 25: *"Je crois que je trouve tranquillement ce que je cherche"*—"I think I am gradually finding what I am looking for."

On the day she met her murderers, sitting near the windmills at the base of Golden Gate Park with their own bulging backpacks and unwashed hair, she must have felt like she was encountering three more like souls. There was Sean Angold, a tall, lanky boy with piercing blue eyes and a dark shock of hair falling into his face; Lila Alligood, a girl with tangled blonde dreadlocks and meth sores on her round cherubic face; and her boyfriend, Haze Lampley, a scruffy-faced and dreadlocked boy with an intensity that failed to meet his eyes. Like her, they were just passing through—somewhere in Oregon, there was a cabin where they planned to start a weed farm and live out their days once they grew tired of wandering and got out of San Francisco.

It was October 2, 2015, an uncharacteristically warm day in San Francisco. Summer in the foggy city doesn't really strike until late September, when for just a few weeks at the beginning of autumn, heat overtakes the usual cool gray that blankets these hills, bright sunlight pushing through the fog and the chill. City dwellers abandon the light jackets that they always carry with them and flock to the city's many outdoor spaces, and the entire region gets overtaken by an endless summer vibe.

According to Sean Angold's testimony, Audrey was shy at first, unsure of how to approach the trio and make the connections she sought in her travels. She passed them on her way to buy beer as they shared a bowl of crystal meth near the windmills in Golden Gate Park.

"Hey, what's up? Want to have some fun?" Haze said they asked her. And she joined them.

~

We will never know for certain what happened during that murderous, drug-fueled week in 2015 that resulted in two killings and three arrests. In my years reporting on crime and mayhem, sitting in on murder trials and poring over court documents, I have learned that truth is relative—there are only the facts and what you believe those facts say, and that varies from person to person.

In any case, we have several accounts of what happened that week: Sean Angold's account, Haze Lampley's account, Lila Alligood's account, and what the investigators and prosecutors believe. Sean was the one to break first, sitting in an interrogation room in Portland, Oregon, and spilling to detectives from both Marin County and San Francisco the details of the murders. His account paints him as the less culpable of the three, which could either be read with a jaded eye as being a bit too convenient, or be accepted as a reasonable explanation for why he talked when the other two did not. But the many investigators involved in the case stand by his account as the truth, pointing out that Lila corroborated his telling of the events. At first, Lila tried to pin both killings on Sean, in an effort to protect her boyfriend, but eventually she cracked after intense questioning. Haze thinks she gave in because she was scared; however, she later bragged to a cellmate in Marin County Jail about the killings, following Sean's narrative to the end. The cellmate, Pamela Bullock, who came forward with the information in hopes of reducing her own sentence, said that Alligood referred to Carey as "the bitch," Marin County Sheriff Detective Scott Buer testified. "All of a sudden, Lampley jumps up and shoots her and there is blood and brains splattered all over," the cellmate said Lila told her.

According to Haze, he and Sean met during one of Haze's many sojourns in San Francisco, in July 2011 in Buena Vista Park, just weeks after my fated meeting with Dave Thompson. Haze was still a teenager and looking for a quiet spot to ingest some methamphetamines in Buena Vista Park. "Street kids call it Tweaker Hill," he said. "If you want to do meth or anything on Haight Street, you go there." And under the park's leafy cover, he encountered Sean, who went by his "dirty kid name" of Smalls—Haze's dirty kid name is just Haze, while Lila's is Māhealani, a remnant from her time living with her family in Hawaii. That day, Haze and Sean gave each other a nod of acknowledgment and would probably have just ignored each other had it not been for a passing policeman doing a walk-through of the area. In having to relocate to another spot, they struck up an easy friendship, bonded mostly by their drug use, and spent the next three days together.

I know from the little that Sean told me in brief phone calls before he stopped responding to my inquiries that his upbringing was not much different from what Haze experienced. Investigators said his family essentially "lived as gypsies" during his early years, before he and his two younger sisters were taken away from their parents in California and entered into the foster care system. His father had been a drug addict and his mother in trouble with the law, Sean said, but his time in foster care was not much of an improvement. He bounced from home to home, some as far out as Texas, before he was adopted by a family in Phelan, California. He balked at reliving the abuses he suffered in foster care, but he did share that one foster parent once almost drowned him as a punishment for getting suspended from school, and that the family that adopted him was psychologically abusive. He was diagnosed as manic-depressive and got into enough trouble as a minor that he was sent off to a group home at sixteen. He ran away, straight into the world of crystal meth.

"There was always this itch in the back of my mind that if I didn't stop doing drugs, something bad would happen," Sean said. "Well, it happened. Unfortunately, it happened in a big way."

Haze said he and Sean never really hung out again after that first meeting, though in the insular world of San Francisco street kids, they must have passed each other on occasion. But the next time they spent any significant amount of time together, their bond would grow beyond that of drugs to one of bloodshed.

According to Sean, it wasn't long after Audrey joined the three that they decided to rob her. They shared cigarettes and drank beer before heading to a nearby 7-Eleven for pizza. "She was foreign and possibly had money," Sean would testify later in court, a Southern twang, a remnant of his time in Texas, still present in his voice. He never specified whose idea it was in the first place, but the plan was to rob her and nothing else, he said.

They whiled away the afternoon together—Sean didn't go into detail about what they did, but her autopsy report found traces of methamphetamine and marijuana in Audrey's system—and returned to the park as night fell, near where they had first met by the windmills. In her lilting Quebecois accent, Audrey thanked them for being her friends, one of her final acts before she was killed. She did not know, in that moment, that Lila had already taken her wallet.

Sean testified that he got up to "take a leak," and when he returned, Lila had lunged across the circle, tackling Audrey to the ground, and was straddling her around her chest. Haze jumped up and hit Audrey on the left side of the face. "What are you doing?" she shouted. But the deserted, leafy confines of Golden Gate Park swallowed her cries.

Golden Gate Park was San Francisco's answer to Central Park. Cutting a green swath through the western portion of the city, the park boasts more of a wildness than its New York counterpart, with much of the 1,017 acres located away from thoroughfares and foot traffic. A person wanting to hide in plain sight could reasonably do so within the boundaries of Golden Gate Park, making it a popular spot for street kids, other factions of the homeless population, and backpackers roughing it on their tour of San Francisco. The park is supposedly closed at night, but more than just the raccoons and coyotes wander around through its trees and bushes after the sun sets.

Hardly Strictly Bluegrass, an annual free music festival held in Golden Gate Park, opened the day of Audrey's murder, but the throngs of people who would have crowded into the park for the free music would have mostly dispersed by the time Audrey found herself in the bushes on the western side of the park, not far from the golf course and the Beach Chalet Soccer Fields. The neighborhoods that surround this area are mostly sleepy and residential, made up of families and surfers, whose close proximity to Ocean Beach made for a lot of early nights in preparation for catching early-morning waves. And that weekend in October is always the city's busiest weekend, with Fleet Week events taking place along the piers located to the northeast. By nightfall, the city's attention would have been turned elsewhere, away from the lush green of the park that would serve as Audrey's mausoleum until a homeless man stumbled upon her body the next morning. No one would have heard when she screamed. No one would have been around to help.

According to Sean, she struggled and fought against Lila and Haze, with Lila still on her chest, trying to tie her hands with a rope. After Sean returned from his bathroom break, he jumped to join the fray, with Lila tossing the rope to him. He worked to tangle the rope around Audrey's flailing legs, while Haze struck her about the face a few times.

And then Haze reached behind him for a camouflage-print pouch.

The night before, the three had decided to go car hopping, which consists of testing door handles on parked cars and making off with any valuables should the car happen to be unlocked. Near the iconic Coit Tower in the Telegraph Hill neighborhood, they hit the ultimate jackpot when it comes to car hopping: in an unlocked Ford F-150, they found a .40-caliber Smith and Wesson handgun, with ammunition, in a camouflage pouch in the console.

Sean said he and Haze would take turns carrying the gun, but most of the time Haze had it in his possession. Haze had a lot of experience with guns, with most of the men in his family being familiar with the weapons and eager to pass on their knowledge to the next generation. Though he identified as a Haight Kid, more a free-living hippie than anything else, Haze said he never traveled without either a big knife or a gun, which he could always easily buy through illegal means for a few hundred dollars.

With Lila still holding Audrey down, Haze introduced the gun into the mix and Audrey panicked, struggling even harder, Sean said. She pleaded, "Please don't shoot me, please don't shoot me," and Haze responded, "Shut up, bitch, or I'll kill you."

And he did. He pulled the trigger with the barrel pointed at her left temple, splattering blood and brain matter everywhere, including onto Lila, who had been looking directly into Audrey's face when Haze took her life. With Lila blocking his view, Sean recalled hearing a pop and not much else.

In his testimony against Lila and Haze, Sean got emotional when he described Audrey's death. Though it was hard to pin down, I got a sense as I watched him on the stand that he was, at the very least, fond of Audrey, and maybe even had romantic inclinations toward her. "I didn't know what was going on," Sean said tearfully.

"She's dead, dude," Haze told him. "Don't worry about it."

~

I spoke with Haze for the first time not long after Sean took a plea deal in exchange for his testimony against Haze and Lila. In pleading guilty to one count of second-degree murder for just Steve Carter's death, Sean presented a version of the killings that put the majority of the responsibility on Haze. But from behind the partition at Marin County Jail, speaking to me through a phone receiver, Haze seemed fairly apathetic when it came to Sean. "Everybody keeps telling me I should be mad at him," he said. "But what's to get mad about? Yeah, he sold me out. He's trying to put all the blame on me and Lila. That shouldn't be anybody's blame. We were all dealt a bad hand."

Two years later, in the visiting room of California Substance Abuse Treatment Facility in Corcoran, Haze was no longer so cavalier. When Haze heard that Sean had been jumped several times in the facility next door, the fate for many prisoners considered to be "snitches," he doubled over in a full-on belly laugh, displaying the most joy I had ever seen from him. "I can't help but laugh," he chuckled. Haze claimed that he knew Smalls had a price on his head, though Haze said he had nothing to do with it—it was because Smalls had outed Haze on the stand as having family ties to the Hells Angels. "I've had people in here offer to take him out for me, and I told them I didn't want anything to do with it," he said.

He said the sympathy from the other inmates comes from "the fact that he blamed it all on me and I only pulled the trigger once." According to Haze, Audrey's death was all Sean's doing.

"He shot her," he said. "He shot the girl. We were just robbing her. She was all tied up and we were gathering her stuff and he just shot her. He said, 'Well, now she definitely can't ID us.'"

In Haze's account of the killing, he and Lila were on their way to the cabin in Oregon when they arrived in San Francisco, just a week or so before the killings.

They promised each other it would be only a quick stop. Haze said he was still avoiding Haight Street at that point, and so they set up shop outside a Safeway near Fisherman's Wharf, panhandling for money to get them north. And there was Smalls. Haze claimed that Sean had to avoid Haight Street too because he was "a shyster." "He would rob and cheat street kids," Haze said. "At least when I got fucked up and robbed people, I did it away from my people, at Fisherman's Wharf or Coit

Tower. Rob the rich people, not the street kids." Sean asked to hang out with the couple, and they agreed.

Sean testified that he had been selling methamphetamines in the years before the killings. According to Haze, after meeting up with Haze and Lila, Sean pulled out a crystal meth pipe. And though Haze and Lila had been off the hard drugs for a few weeks at that point, since they had started their journey north, they couldn't say no.

Because it had been weeks since he had done anything that hard, Haze said the drugs affected him more than usual and he stayed high for the days he was in San Francisco. When Audrey strayed into their path on October 2, he was still feeling it. And they kept smoking meth, he said, while also smoking pot with Audrey. "I was out there," he said. "I was staring out into space. I was talking to myself. I was gone." He can't remember anything about Audrey, but he remembered that at some point that afternoon, they met up with a man from Humboldt County, California, who had smoked them out and gave Audrey the creeps by hitting on her. He remembered that Sean had been hitting on her too—Sean had been growing tired of being Haze and Lila's third wheel—and that Lila had also made advances, which was how she got Audrey's wallet. Like Sean, Haze can't remember whose idea it had been to rob her, but when somebody brought up the idea, "I was like, 'OK.' I have nothing against robbing people. Robbing people is how we survive." They had robbed a drug dealer at gunpoint just before they had met Audrey. Haze justified that robbery in that this man had been selling "crap weed" to street kids, but it wasn't the first time he'd robbed someone, nor would it be the last.

They eventually made their way to the bushes to set up camp for the night. According to Haze, he and Sean both got up to pee, and when he returned, Lila was sitting on Audrey's legs and "Smalls had a gun to her neck."

"So we're in it now," he said. "We tie her up, and the entire time, we were saying, 'Where's the money?' We knew she had money."

Audrey was squirming and saying no, and at one point managed to hit Lila, which was why Haze "socked her." According to her autopsy report, Audrey had a fractured nose and scrapes on her scalp, jaw, neck, chin, and lower back. They were getting ready to leave, Haze said, when he heard "a pop."

"I fucking shot her, bro," Sean said.

"What? Why?" Haze asked.

"Now she can't ID us."

"I was like, 'Holy shit, dude,'" Haze said. "OK, we need to go."

They brought Audrey's belongings to Ocean Beach and went through them, throwing away what they didn't want. Haze noticed he had some of her blood on his hand from when he'd hit her, and he washed it off with some water from a water bottle. They came across a "drunk couple," Haze said, and when they asked whether the couple had anything for them to drink, the couple gave them a two-liter bottle of soda and a bag of pretzels.

The three went back into the park to find another place to sleep. They hunkered down in a little area near the baseball fields in the eastern part of the park, but were awakened early by a parks worker. They went to the Starbucks at Ninth Avenue and Irving Street, and each of them got large Frappuccinos that they paid for with the money they took from Audrey—Haze had a venti Java Chip Frappuccino with an extra shot of espresso and caramel drizzle, to be exact. Lila tried to use Audrey's credit card at a Jamba Juice, and when it didn't work, they got rid of it. Investigators later found a debit card belonging to Audrey Carey at Lucky 13, a dive bar in the Castro neighborhood, but Haze denied ever going there.

Even if Haze's version of events were true and he didn't pull the trigger, he still witnessed a murder. He would have seen the blood and brain matter splattered about, the blood and brain matter of someone with whom he had shared weed and a meal and conversation over the course of several hours. But in his recollection of the killing, he seemed incredibly indifferent about a life having been taken. All of them did. Minutes after they killed her, they were snacking on pretzels and soda on the beach. They slept soundly in another part of the park. They woke up the next morning and got Starbucks. According to Haze, he and Lila were so nonchalant about Audrey's death that when they learned about the free music festival, they wanted to go back and enjoy it.

In the visitation room at the California Substance Abuse Treatment Facility in Corcoran, I found myself repeatedly circling back to the aftermath of Audrey's murder, cajoling and at times almost begging Haze for some kind of reaction. She had spent hours with them before they killed her, and she considered them her friends according to Sean's testimony, which meant their time together had to have been somewhat significant.

"What do you remember about her?" I asked. *Was she kind, was she curious? Was she happy, was she sweet? Was she scared when you held her down and tied her up with rope? Did she know she was going to die when you pulled out the gun?*

"I didn't have any interest in her," Haze said. "I didn't really talk to her. It was mostly Māhealani and Smalls." Later, after more prodding, he recalled that she had a slight accent that he thought was midwestern, that she "looked like a country corn-fed girl," and that she carried with her a giant bag of baby carrots.

Even though his account of her killing differed from what investigators believed to have happened, he still witnessed a bloodshed. He still hit a young girl in the face, hard enough to get her blood on his knuckles, and then watched a bullet pierce her temple just moments later. He would have seen her blood and her brain matter splattered around her, the blood and brain matter of someone with whom he had whiled away an afternoon, sharing weed and a meal and conversation. *Something,* I implored, *anything. You had to have felt something.* But each time I pushed, he responded with the same blank stare.

"Smalls got super paranoid," he said. "I think it was fucking with him." But it wasn't fucking with Haze and Lila, and Haze didn't think there was anything amiss with them reacting this way. It's been like this for almost his whole life, he said—the flat affect, the inability to process emotions. But most of all, he said, their life experiences have numbed them. "People who have been tortured and been through the things we've been through have been desensitized to a lot," he said.

This sort of desensitization is not unusual among the street kid population. If their former lives hadn't scarred them beyond feeling, their time on the streets, fighting to survive, would have. Nothing could shock them anymore because of what they had endured.

And according to Haze, that all began for him from almost the moment he was born.

FOUR

Haze believes he was conceived in a flophouse on Broderick Street in San Francisco, a claim his mother, Mindi Bowman, thoroughly disputes. "It was our apartment in Portland," she insisted. "We called it the 'Morrison Hotel' because we had this poster that was the Morrison Hotel from the Doors. It was '$2.50 a night and up,'" Mindi said, a reference to the sign perched in front of lead singer Jim Morrison on this particular album cover. "There were quite a few of us in that apartment, and that was where he was conceived. We named him Morrison for Jim Morrison, and Haze for 'Purple Haze.'"

No matter the city of his conception, Haze told me that he has felt a certain connection to San Francisco his entire life. While he can't remember much of his early years, he was brought up in the same hippie, traveling lifestyle that his mother had as a child—the sort of lifestyle once celebrated in San Francisco.

"We went to Grateful Dead shows and lived in communal living," Mindi said. "My mom was a hippie chick and my dad was a biker, and that was what I knew. My first home was a school bus. It was just like a big family. You raise your children together, and whoever had a strong point with the kids was who was with the kids."

This existence is anything but stable, but Haze has no bad memories of this time spent with his mother, his younger half brother, and his mother's various boyfriends. Not long after Haze's birth in July 1992, his mother and father began following the Grateful Dead on tour, along with another couple that they would each eventually pair off with after ending their own relationship. For his first five years, Haze and his family drifted along the West Coast. They weren't exactly homeless during this period, just sometimes voluntarily houseless, sleeping in vehicles, campers, or RVs, or sometimes just tents.

Mindi said while her kids were young, all she really did was smoke weed and drink the occasional beer, but the bits and pieces of Haze's childhood memories that flash forth in passing conversation say otherwise. There were the psychedelics—when Haze was fourteen months old, somebody had put LSD on sugar cubes, and he gobbled up three before the adults could stop him. He doesn't believe there were any long-term effects—"I was the happiest they had ever seen me," he laughed—but the work his mother's boyfriend was doing in manufacturing these psychedelics suggests they were more prolific during these years than Mindi originally let on. Their little family was always popular among the Deadheads for this reason, Haze said.

Haze remembers going up to Oregon, to the family cabin, as well as living for some time "in a little red house" in North Plains, next door to his mother's father and stepmother—Grandpa and Grandma Cloud, to Haze. He had been around five then, his mother said. The family had a pit bull named Zeus that was so protective over Haze that it would chase after the school bus when he left for school.

His grandfather was still drinking heavily then, and his mother was using during this time, he said, all of which led to several serious car crashes with him as a passenger. They were awful wrecks that involved the car flipping over, and he remembers that it was always because the driver was either high or drunk. He can't remember who the drivers were, but the only options at that time were his grandpa, his mother, or her boyfriends. Mindi claims she never got in a wreck with him, but to this day, Haze said he remains terrified of driving and stays asleep when he's in a car.

In reality, Haze hadn't spent much time in San Francisco at all. When he was seven, his father took custody, and Haze moved across the country to live with him, his stepmother, another half brother, and his stepsister. After what Haze described as three traumatic and abuse-filled years there, he returned to his mother, who was living in San Diego. He spent his adolescence bouncing between her home, the streets before and after she became homeless, and in and out of other Southern California juvenile hall facilities, before a stint in the Pacific Northwest and then his life on the road.

~

Fredericksburg, Virginia

Haze and his mother both say Virginia was where Haze's fate was sealed. The trauma he allegedly sustained in the three years he spent with his father was a turning point; it was what irrevocably set him on the path to bloodshed and heartbreak. It was here that he turned to hard drugs to escape his reality, the start of many years of addiction and self-medication, and it was here that his behavioral issues reached an apex, resulting in the first of many mental health diagnoses.

But despite these assertions, we may never know for certain what occurred there. Much of Haze's memories up until the age of twelve or so have seemingly been blocked out or distorted, either from trauma or from extensive drug use. Even his mother doesn't know for sure what Haze went through from the ages of seven to ten. "There are things that happened that only Haze and his father and his stepmother know," Mindi said. "They cut off all ties and communication I had with Haze when he was in Virginia. It wasn't until he was ten, almost eleven, that his father called and said he'd pay for his plane ticket back and that he just didn't want to take care of him anymore. He called him the spawn of Satan."

Neither his father nor his stepmother responded to my inquiries, but Haze's paternal grandmother, speaking on his father's behalf, staunchly denied all of Mindi and Haze's allegations, saying that "almost all of what they allege is not true and should not be printed as it is just scandalizing slander and not factual material, whether it's alleged or not." As no one on Haze's paternal side of the family has been criminally convicted of any wrongdoing against him, and no one wishes to have any further connection to him in the public realm, I am not naming anyone on this side of the family.

According to Mindi, Haze's paternal grandmother "tricked me into signing temporary custody over to her," purely out of spite. By taking Haze out of the state, they were able to lie to family court to allow for permanent custody. Haze's grandmother says Mindi was "never tricked" and that Mindi had asked her to take temporary custody of Haze because she "was coming down from being so strung out on drugs she could barely function and take care of herself let alone two small, active boys who had some serious acting-out behaviors." She disputes Mindi and Haze's account, saying that Haze lived in his father's custody from age seven to right before his twelfth birthday, during which time he was allowed phone calls with Mindi.

The grandmother claims that Haze knew he was going to live in Virginia with his father, stepmother, and younger half brother and stepsister, but according to Haze, the move came as a shock to which he could not adjust. As unstable as his life was with Mindi and her boyfriends, with their drug use and nomadic lifestyles, he loved her, and suddenly, he said, his father and grandmother were telling him that she had abandoned him. That he was in this unfamiliar place, thousands of miles from the landscapes he grew up in, because she didn't want him. And then, he said, his father began entering his bedroom at night and raping him.

Only two people can know whether these allegations of rape are true: Haze and his father. A traumatized boy with behavioral issues who blocked out years of his childhood from his memory—and had a warped relationship to the truth—and a man who didn't respond to my inquiries. Though Haze's grandmother denied these accusations on Haze's father's behalf, the problem with sexual assault is that even if his father had set up a face-to-face meeting, looked me in the eye, and sworn under oath that no such rape had ever taken place, that still doesn't mean it didn't happen. As we've unfortunately had to learn with the #MeToo movement, far too often it's the victim's word against the alleged perpetrator's, with no independent way to verify either. Cases of intrafamilial sexual abuse involving children are particularly difficult to prove, according to the Center for Sex Offender Management, with the perpetrator imposing a level of secrecy around the abuse that the child is unwilling or too scared to breach.

While Haze's half brother remembers "being terrified" of Haze, he cannot recall any instances of sexual abuse. "My dad was in the military for a good portion of my childhood, so I honestly couldn't account for anything he would've done," he said. "He may have been an asshole with little affection for his kids, but he never touched me or my sister in the ten or so years I remember him."

Once again, this neither absolves their father of wrongdoing, nor does it confirm Haze's account. It's not uncommon for family child molesters to limit their abuse, grooming and isolating just one child from the rest of the family. It's not beyond the realm of possibility that the half brother, who at the time was not even four years old, wouldn't have been able to comprehend it if something awful was happening to someone close to him. Studies show that preschool-age children can mimic and mirror another person's emotions but cannot yet understand what they are or process why they feel that way.

Further complicating matters, Haze's grandmother said that Haze's behavior during his time in Virginia had temporarily broken up his father's marriage, forcing his father to move back to Washington with Haze for a few years. Haze's telling of this time period has him only in Virginia, but his recollections are foggy at best. He remembers his father coming into his bedroom to molest him, sometimes as often as two or three times a week. He remembers his father threatening to make him "disappear" if he told anyone about the rape, and he remembers believing that this strong military man could and would make good on that threat. He remembers that beyond the alleged rape, his father acted very aloof toward him, except when it came time to impart harsh discipline—making him scrub the kitchen floor with a toothbrush, forcing him to stand in the corner with his arms raised to shoulder height while holding weights in each hand—punishments Haze had to adhere to, or he'd get the belt. Haze's grandmother said his father would have him sit in the corner holding books for discipline, but that was the extent of it.

Other than these vague recollections, Haze said he has only three distinct memories from his time in Virginia. One is of a large spider at a community garden that he smashed to death with a shovel. And another is the psychological abuse he inflicted on his half brother. They had been standing in an open field during a lightning storm, and Haze told the terrified boy to run for a nearby tree. Even though he knew that was not what you were supposed to do during a lightning storm, he lied and told the boy that the only way to stay safe was to climb a big tree. Haze remembers his brother running for the tree and collapsing in a fit of hysterical tears. Lightning had struck the tree, Haze said, just before his brother had reached it.

The half brother was three and a half years younger than Haze, but even at such a young age, he remembers feeling disturbed by things Haze did, to both him and his sister. He declined to go into detail about what those acts were, but Haze readily copped to "torturing" his half brother and stepsister. He hurt them physically and also played mind games with them, he said. "Like I said, I was a fucked-up kid." He shrugged.

According to Haze and his mother, Virginia was where the hurt began for Haze, but according to his younger half brother, it was here that Haze began hurting others as well. "I couldn't grasp why he would be so violent and careless," he said.

Haze knows he acted out while he was in Virginia. He ran away, assaulted his father and stepmother, and wreaked havoc in their home however he could. He didn't try to justify his behavior, but said it was the only way he knew to express his anger and confusion at the pain and betrayal he carried with him.

"I was angry at the world," he said. "I wanted to hurt people, so I turned that inside. I burned myself with cigarettes, cut myself, got into fights."

Growing up the way he had with Mindi, following the Grateful Dead on tour and basically doing whatever he wanted, he didn't respond well to this new environment. His stepmother, who Haze said he believed did her best with him, got him into therapy, even going so far as to have several family sessions. When he was nine, Haze said, Child Protective Services took him in for a mental health evaluation, and he was diagnosed with schizoaffective disorder and post-traumatic stress disorder.

According to his grandmother, Haze wasn't diagnosed with schizoaffective disorder until he was a teenager in juvenile hall on a drug charge. When he was seven, he had been diagnosed with attention deficit hyperactivity disorder, and had been taking Ritalin when he arrived in Virginia, where he was diagnosed with depression and placed on medication for that.

"He was hard to control and willful, among other behaviors, and was easily angered," she said. "He often took his behavior out on family members. It took them a while with mental health assistance to get his behavior under control."

While we may never be able to verify the specifics of the rape and abuse allegations, Haze's behavior in the years that followed suggests that he had, at some point during his childhood, experienced trauma and been abused sexually. According to the National Child Traumatic Stress Network, children exposed to complex trauma may display impairment with impulse control, aggression, self-destructive behavior, and substance abuse. They may attempt to communicate their traumatic past in a reen-actment in their day-to-day behavior. Haze's hypersexuality—he said he began fooling around with other neighborhood kids pretty much immediately after he arrived in Virginia, and was having sex with young girls while living on the streets in San Diego when he was twelve—and his malicious behavior toward his younger siblings all match the behavior of a child abuse victim.

And then there was the drug use. Some studies have found that teens with a history of childhood sexual abuse tend to demonstrate a three- to fourfold increase in the rate of substance dependency com-pared to their teen counterparts with no history of childhood sexual abuse. Haze said he had only three distinct memories of Virginia, and his third and final was when he was ten. An older neighbor, a sixteen-year-old kid, offered to teach him how to snort heroin. They were a street or two away from his father's house, closer to where the other kid lived, and just sitting on the sidewalk. The kid showed him the right amount to snort. And that was it. "The pain went away," Haze said.

~

Although Haze puts the blame on his father, his half brother said the sexual abuse started when Haze lived with his mother. "Before he came to our family in Virginia, he was beaten and pimped out by his mom and her boyfriend so that they could afford drugs," he said. The half brother said, "the entire other half of the family can attest to" this abuse taking place, that Mindi and her boyfriends locked Haze and his brother in a closet for days on end so they could get high.

"Mindi is no saint," the half brother said. "His time in Virginia was probably the best time in his life as far as actually having a family that cared for him, and getting the help he needed for his illness."

Mindi denied these allegations, and, as usual, Haze stood by his mother. While he acknowledged the gaps in his memory, especially in his early years, he said his mom "gave him a pretty good childhood," even with her drug addiction and chronic homelessness. He said he thinks he would remember getting pimped out for drugs. He has a distinct memory of the older daughter of his mom's abusive boyfriend at the family cabin in Oregon, making him show her his penis and touching it, which he doesn't consider sexual abuse because he doesn't believe children can sexually abuse each other. And even if his mom's abusive boyfriend used to lock him and his younger brother up in their closet-size room, it wasn't so they could do drugs. "If my mom wanted to do drugs, her dealers would go to her," he said. "They were mostly her boyfriends."

His grandmother and father would tell him a lot of lies about his mother, he said, to poison him against her. And for some time, they worked. He thinks that's why his half brother believes that it was his mother who was at fault.

Once they were reunited, Mindi had asked Haze what had happened in Virginia. "But he would get so upset when I would try to talk to him that we would leave it alone instead of bringing it up," she said. "There was one time he got really upset, and I said, 'Just tell me what's going on.' He couldn't process the fact that his dad had tried to kill him basically. All I could do was hold him and tell him, 'You're safe here. We never have to see him again if you don't want to.'"

Though she doesn't know for certain what her son experienced in his father's home, Mindi can imagine. She remembered the three years she spent with him, from ages sixteen to nineteen. She remembered his growing dependency on heroin and alcohol and his manipulative ways of mentally and emotionally abusing her. "He would make me feel like

I was a piece of shit," she said. "He would make me feel like I was no good. He would attack me as a person until I felt like this tiny little nothing inside."

Haze's grandmother said she never saw "any abuse, emotional, verbal, or physical," between her son and Mindi, which is exactly what you'd expect a mother to say about her son. According to Haze's grandmother, Haze's father never did hard drugs and never had an alcohol problem, and he worked to support Mindi and Haze in the brief time they lived together. Though Haze's half brother supported Mindi's assessment of his father when he described him as "an asshole with little affection for his kids," Haze's grandmother said that sounded like a line the half brother's mother, her son's other ex, had fed him. She had few kind words to spare for Mindi or Haze, and claimed that their account of "the horrible life he wants everyone to believe he lived growing up" was just his way to continue victimizing others "so he doesn't have to take responsibility for his own behavior and actions."

Mindi wasn't surprised to hear that Haze had acted out from the moment he had arrived in his father's home. Though he returned to her a different boy than the one she'd raised, she saw in him an anger that she understood all too well.

"They took him away from me and that was all he really knew," she said. "Me or anybody else in my family, you take us away from our comfort, we become violent. That is how we deal with our emotion."

It's been decades since Haze's half brother last saw him—and that's more than all right with him. "As far as I am concerned, I never really knew him, nor do I want to," he said.

"You want to understand how people like him end up on the street at a young age?" Haze's half brother asked when I first reached out to him on Facebook. "They do it to themselves. They refuse help at every turn, mentally ill or not. You can't force someone into a life they don't want to live, and troubled adolescents do not give a fuck about their surroundings or the people that surround them."

"He had more than a few opportunities to get better and solve his situation, but chose not to, and you see where it ended up."

And unfortunately, he said, in a way, he and his family expected something like this to happen when it came to Haze. "When you lack empathy, you're capable of literally anything," he said. "We were always concerned that he would hurt somebody."

FIVE

Old Railroad Grade Fire Road
Marin County, California

In all his travels around California, Haze had somehow managed to bypass Marin County entirely. Though just over the Golden Gate Bridge from the city of his birth, the scenic shorelines, lush redwoods, hale outdoors-enthusiast vibe, and affluent family-friendly suburbs of Marin County don't exactly attract street kids like Haze—and for the few that end up stumbling through, they don't stay long enough to form the sort of communities that exist across the bridge. In fact, Haze, Lila, and Sean seemed so out of place in Marin County that a woman called the police and took a photo of them just hours before Steve Carter's murder. "She said they made her feel uncomfortable," Marin County Sheriff Deputy Salma Tijero testified. "She said they appeared grungy and traveling through the area."

"I had no idea a place like that existed," Haze said. But it was here that Lokita and Steve Carter sought refuge as they faced down what Lokita believed then would be the most difficult battle of their seventeen-year relationship: breast cancer. She couldn't have known, when they left their dream home in Costa Rica and moved in with friends in August 2015 so that she could undergo chemotherapy, that in just a few months, her life would be upended by a more insidious force than cancer.

Theirs was a late-in-life love story, a deep and soulful devotion based on common philosophies and aspirations. Both respected and well-established instructors in tantra, the Carters met at Harbin Hot Springs, a clothing-optional resort north of Napa. Within a year of their fateful meeting, they founded the Ecstatic Living Institute, within which they organized countless seminars, workshops, and retreats around their tantric teachings.

Lokita had started a blog to document her cancer treatment, but after Steve's murder, it turned into almost an instructional tome on how to survive loss and grief under the most trying of circumstances. She wrote in depth about the blissful years she had had with Steve, years filled with laughter, adventure, activity, meditation, friendship, and love. They had traveled far and wide together, sometimes to teach at tantra workshops but more often than not for fun. They had celebrated birthdays in places like Kathmandu and Las Vegas, surrounded by friends old and new—the couple seemed to strike up friendships everywhere they went—and always had a community that loved and rallied around them. They had visited with his adult children, Emily and Rob, who lived in California, and ridden motorcycles along the beach. For almost a year before his murder, they had lived in peace in Costa Rica, with their sweet Doberman pinscher, Coco, whom Lokita lovingly referred to as their "doghter."

The day of his murder—October 5, 2015—was yet another beautiful day in Marin County. Lokita last saw Steve in the garden of their friends' home in San Geronimo, about four miles from the popular trail near Fairfax where Steve would take his last breaths. Steve was an active man and loved to take Coco out into nature. Before her treatment, Lokita would usually have joined them, but her body grew tired too often with the chemotherapy. Steve had wanted her to go on a walk on the beach, she wrote, but she had declined, believing there to be hundreds more walks on the beach with her beloved in the future. She snapped one last photo of him in the garden before he and Coco got into the couple's silver Volkswagen Jetta, purchased just months earlier to bring Lokita to her cancer treatment, and headed toward Fairfax. He texted her at 5:42 p.m., saying he would pick her up for a meditation session at a nearby center. But just minutes later, Steve and Coco would encounter three young, unwashed kids on the trail, and Lokita would never hear from Steve again.

In his account of events, Sean displayed the same sort of memory problems that Haze has, especially around the concept of time. But according to Sean, he separated from Haze and Lila for a brief period after Audrey's killing. He recalled going to a Subway in the Castro neighborhood and trying to use her credit card there, only to have it fail, and then jumping a turnstile at the BART station to go to Berkeley. When he made it back to San Francisco, he met up with Haze and Lila again at Fisherman's Wharf. He had heard them talking about their plan to go to the cabin in Oregon in the days they had spent together, and now, with a body in Golden Gate Park, the getaway felt more necessary than ever.

They stopped by the Safeway, where they stole food and a bottle of Fireball Whisky, and then made their way over the bridge to Vista Point in Marin County. They spent the night there, and continued on to Sausalito, a seaside Fabergé egg of a town with miles of cute little bars and eateries, shops for tourists, and breathtaking views of San Francisco. They wasted most of the day away lounging around the water fountain in the city's downtown stretch, eating sandwiches they bought at a deli with money they got from selling LSD to tourists. Sean boosted an expensive bright-colored bicycle, and they headed down a bike path, where they slept that night. The next morning, they kept following the path and ended up stuck in a residential area, unsure of how to find a main roadway to continue north.

It was Haze's idea, Sean said, to not just rob someone for their car keys, but to also shoot them. It was taking too long to get out of Marin County, and despite their best efforts, the three hitchhikers had not yet found a ride. Sean tried trading the bicycle he had stolen for a ride north, but no one took him up on the offer.

They had made it to Sir Francis Drake Boulevard, one of Marin's main arterial roadways, and sat in a turnout, contemplating their next move. A silver Volkswagen Jetta slowed by their turnout, but the driver—Steve Carter—"looked at us like we were crazy," said Sean, and continued on to another place to park. It was Lila who chose Steve as their target, Sean explained, taking note of his white hair and his age. Another man had walked by them with a long-haired dog, but "we all came to the conclusion that he was too young," Sean said.

They walked onto the trail and waited for him to return. Haze had the gun the entire time, Sean said. While Haze and Lila stayed closer to the road, Sean started walking the bicycle farther down the trail, passing Steve on his way out with Coco. "I heard someone say, 'What are you doing?' And then I heard a shot," he testified.

While Haze remained unfazed by Audrey's murder, writing it off as something in which he had only the most tertiary involvement, talking about Steve gave him just the briefest moments of pause. "The old dude kind of fucked with me," he said, meaning that killing Steve had affected him.

"I said, 'Look dude, we have to rob you,'" Haze said.

"Why?" Steve asked.

"Because my friend is an idiot and we need to get out of the state."

Long before they had reached this point, Haze and Lila had gotten fed up with Sean. They were coming down from their high and were irritable, Haze said, so technically they were fed up with everybody and everything, but Sean was freaking out in the hours after Audrey's murder and it grated on the couple.

According to Haze, Sean never parted ways with them. They went to the Subway in the Castro, but Sean was talking crazy. "We were fucking starving, and stoned," Haze said, "and his bright idea was to try and rob the Subway." They wasted away the rest of the day in Dolores Park. "Half the day, we went back to sleep," he said. "We were still hella coming down. And then we got more drugs and got up. And then we got some psychedelics and got even more up."

They got those drugs at Fisherman's Wharf, having hopped on Muni to get there. A friend of theirs had told them about the Hardly Strictly Bluegrass festival still happening in Golden Gate Park, and Haze and Lila wanted to go back. "Smalls starts freaking out," Haze said. "He was like, 'They're going to find it, oh my god, we've got to get out of San Francisco.' But I was like, 'Dude, do you know how many people disappear in Golden Gate Park?'"

But they headed toward the Golden Gate Bridge, arguing the entire time. "We kept going back and forth, like, 'Dude, we got a gun, we can just use it to get a car, pop the guy in the trunk, and then let him out when it's time to ditch the car,'" Haze said. "That would be the best way to rob somebody. Nobody could call the cops because they'd be with us."

For as heated as he and Lila could get with each other, Haze said they only really fought when they were coming down from a high. By that point, they had walked over the bridge and set up camp at Vista Point in Marin County, he and Lila tussling the entire time over who was hogging the blanket and who was poking whom in their sleep.

When they woke up, Haze said, they were still feeling awful, but they ran into some college kids on the bridge and sold them fake LSD for about thirty dollars. They saw a bicyclist head down a bike path and realized there was a way to continue north without having to walk on the narrow shoulder of Highway 101 and through the rainbow Robin Williams Tunnel. They ended up in Sausalito, where Sean stole some food and they bought sandwiches with the money they got from selling the fake drugs. Sean boosted the bicycle, and after they got directions from another homeless person they met downtown, they continued down the bike path again, where they bunked down for the night.

A bicyclist woke them up the next morning, telling them that children were going to start heading to school near there so they had to leave. Here, Haze's account matched Sean's in that they got stuck in a residential area before eventually making their way to Sir Francis Drake Boulevard. As soon as they hit the main thoroughfare, all three had their thumbs out, trying to get a ride north. They stopped for a break at the first turnout, Sean still annoying Haze and Lila with his constant harassment of passersby, trying to exchange the bicycle for a ride with people who already had bicycles. "Smalls was on people about it," he said. "He was literally asking everybody he could for a ride. By this time, we were hella regretting taking him out of San Francisco."

Haze's recollection also matched Sean's, insisting it was Lila who chose Steve as their target. "Māhealani remembered that car, that it belonged to that old guy with the brown dog," Haze said. "She said we can just go back down and wait for him to come back and rob him for his car. We were going to first ask him for a ride."

The sun was about to set. The trio went down the trail, stashed their gear in the bushes, and just waited. They relaxed. "I know I was like laid out on my back," Haze said. "Smalls had taken his bike behind the tree." They sat there, "just chilling" and rerolling some cigarettes, waiting for the man who they, in the best-case scenario, were just going to point a gun at, but were willing to shoot if the worst-case scenario should come to fruition.

Haze was fairly cavalier up to this point, laughing about how absurd Sean was acting and smiling at how irritable he and Lila would get when they were coming down from a high. But he paused ever so slightly when recounting Steve's murder.

However, it was also at this point that his account started to elbow and stretch at the already threadbare limits of his credibility. According to Haze, the shooting was an accident—but he also wouldn't have hesitated to shoot Steve had he tried anything.

Lila and Sean "started getting in an argument about who would actually rob him," Haze said. "I told them they didn't want me to do it because if I did it and he said no, I'd pull the trigger."

Although Haze's girlfriend had marked Steve as their target because he was old, Haze recognized that he was athletic and fit. Haze said he assumed that despite his age, he would know how to disarm a person and fight back. Without question, Haze said, "I would have shot him if he tried something."

"You guys know how I am," he said he told Lila and Sean. "If I set myself to something, I'm the type of person that, no matter what, will do whatever it takes to get it done."

But they wouldn't stop arguing, and Haze, already annoyed, grabbed the gun.

"Even with my brain moving and racing in a million different directions, I've always had a sort of eye-of-the-hurricane calm," Haze said. "And he was getting away."

Steve was just putting the leash back onto Coco when he saw Haze. He was so close to the end of the trail. He was so close to making it to the road unscathed. He was so close to the car, where he would have hustled Coco into the back before hopping behind the wheel. So close to turning the key in the ignition and circling back on Sir Francis Drake Boulevard, so close to making it home to Lokita, whom he could have woken with a kiss so they'd make it to their meditation session, or whom he could have lain next to and allowed to have a few more moments of rest. So close to seeing her make a full recovery from the cancer, to returning to their home in Costa Rica. So close to watching his only daughter get married, to walking her down the aisle. "He was getting away," Haze said, and he almost did. Steve Carter was so close to making it out alive.

Haze said he told Steve that they just wanted his car keys and cell phone, that if he just waited for the next person to come along with a phone, he could call for help and get a ride back. But Haze said that he saw Steve instead hit the emergency button on his phone.

"I moved to stop him," he said, "but I was wearing these Jesus sandals. I tripped, and I pulled the trigger."

Had Steve only sustained one gunshot wound, Haze's recollection would be believable. But three bullets struck Steve, according to the county coroner—one that entered at his right jaw and exited on the left side of his head, one that went through his abdomen, and a third that pierced his thigh. One bullet struck Coco through her eye. And Haze himself admitted that he emptied the clip. Minus the bullet that killed Audrey Carey, that could mean anywhere from seven to fourteen rounds for a .40-caliber Smith and Wesson handgun.

The gun was a semiautomatic weapon, meaning somebody would have to actively pull the trigger again and again and again in order to empty the clip. While there are hundreds of YouTube tutorials on how to convert a semiautomatic handgun to be fully automatic, investigators testified that the gun was in perfect working order and had no modifications to it. And if the gun had had this surprise modification, then it would be safe to assume that Audrey too would have sustained more than just one bullet wound.

Still, Haze stands by this account. "Nobody believes me when I say that," he said. "But it was like a mechanical reaction. If I didn't grab it, the gun would have flown out of my hand and he could have gotten it and we would have been arrested."

"I didn't want to shoot him," he insisted. "I didn't." But even if he hadn't wanted to, Haze admitted that he would have shot Steve had he fought back in any way. He went into the robbery thinking that Steve could fight back, knowing full well that he would have considered any defensive maneuver to be an attack on himself and Lila, and therefore any response in kind to be an act of defending himself and the girl he loved.

It may have been an accident, but he was ready to kill. "Fuck," Haze remembered thinking, standing there looking at the gun in his hand. The next thing he recalled was Lila and Sean running toward him. "Smalls yelled, 'Find the keys. Go through his fucking pockets, man. Find the keys,'" Haze said. He snapped out of it, and smashed Steve's cell phone onto the ground to destroy it. He rifled through Steve's pockets as he lay bleeding in the dirt and grabbed both his wallet and car keys. Steve still held Coco's leash in his hand. When the first responders came upon the scene, Coco, ever loyal and steadfast, stood guard over her master's body, blood dripping from the eye she would eventually lose.

But Haze didn't see any of that. He, Lila, and Sean raced to the car and threw their belongings in the back. Lila jumped behind the wheel, and Sean in the back seat, while Haze sat in the passenger seat. It wasn't until they were moving, Haze said, that he realized he still had the gun and Steve's bullet-pierced wallet clutched in his blood-covered hands.

He handed the gun to Sean, who pulled out the clip and discarded it out the car window, toward the shoulder and the ditch alongside. He went through Steve's wallet, pulling out the torn and bloody cash and tossing the wallet out the passenger window, which is why it was later found.

Haze fully admits that there are significant gaps in his memory, especially during the period of time between Steve's killing and the moment the three were arrested outside a soup kitchen in Portland, Oregon. "I'm still trying to change time," he said. "Your brain tries to organize things in a way that makes sense to you. Some things stay the same, but some details change." In Portland's Multnomah County Jail, as he awaited his extradition to Marin County, all he could remember was the first gunshot, looking at the gun in his hand, and then being in the car. His ears were ringing for days, and every time he nodded to sleep in the jail cell, he would jerk awake, thinking he heard gunshots.

But from the moment the first bullet hit Steve Carter on October 5, 2015, the three had only one objective in their minds: Get to the car. Get in. Get the hell out of California. Get to the cabin in Oregon. Escape.

SIX

Ocean Beach
San Diego, California

After Virginia, Haze moved back in with Mindi. They lived with her newest boyfriend and his two kids in Lakeside, a small community located about twenty-five minutes away from San Diego. But Haze said he spent most of his time bouncing between Ocean Beach, where he ran wild with a group of street kids like him, and juvenile hall. Mindi would eventually join him on the streets, living out of her car and working at a neighborhood Subway.

When people think of California, they most likely picture something similar to San Diego's Ocean Beach. Sand stretches out along the coast under an impossibly blue sky, and surfers paddle into waves that lap at the shore, squinting in the bright sunlight. Barefoot hippies strum their guitars and sell homemade crafts along the pier, as parents push their strollers past the tourists posing for their quintessential "Cali" photo.

Unhappiness has no place here, in this land of endless summer and good vibes. Faces seem to be frozen in a constant light smile beneath reflective sunglasses. Tourists sport T-shirts advertising their favorite new beach or bar, or maybe blaring with tie-dye patterns in a weird paean to the region's hippie culture. Joggers and cyclists joust with pedestrians along the boardwalk. Everyone looks healthy, even those who are grotesquely overweight or heroin-addict thin. Complete strangers stop on the sidewalks to pet passing dogs and make conversation with others who just happen to be in the same place at the right time. But it's here that travelers and dirty kids from around the country congregate, and with them, the physical and emotional baggage that they carry at all times.

Almost every traveling street kid I've met has passed through Ocean Beach at some point. On the online message boards, subreddits, and social media groups for travelers, dirty kids, and train hoppers, everyone speaks highly of Ocean Beach. "Head for Ocean Beach," one person posted in the vagabond subreddit. "That's where all the street kids and traveling folk go. Ask where the dunes are, and that's where you should sleep. The cops won't fuck with you there, but they will on the beach in the morning. Eventually you'll meet some travelers that will take you in and show you the ropes."

Just blocks from cafés selling five-dollar nut mylk lattes, brunch spots billing bottomless mimosas, and craft beer eateries with sunbaked outdoor patios, these kids can hide in plain sight, blending in with all the other beach bums. In the light of day, they can pass for anybody else. They could be dirty, their hair clumped in unwashed chunks, or they could be one of the free-living locals wearing their hair in dreadlocks. They could be strung out or sleeping off a hangover under a palm tree, or they could be just one of the many beachgoers relaxing in the perfect weather.

And when dusk hits, they disappear into the shadows, fading into the crowd that gathers to watch the sunset. They can be loud and raucous and pass as just one of the many incorrigible youth, gallivanting through the sand and hurrying home before curfew. They can bundle up in their blankets and hoodies against the sharp ocean breeze and look like any of the many soaking in the last bits of yet another perfect beach day. They can be their own weird, damaged selves and be accepted.

One chilly morning with the wind howling in from the ocean in frigid gusts that pierced through your clothing and into your very core, Jonny "Indigenous" Hurst struggled to clear the roadway of dead fronds that had detached themselves from palm trees in the night. "Just another beautiful morning in Ocean Beach!" he called out as a greeting.

Jonny has been houseless, not homeless, on and off for the past twenty years, and even though he was born in Tulsa, he calls Ocean Beach his hometown—Ocean Beach, he said, not San Diego. There's a level of kindness extended to the homeless and traveling population here that I haven't seen in many other places—the baristas at the café that sells five-dollar nut mylk lattes give out cups of coffee when they can to the kids who ask. Even though they're not supposed to, they let a man who has been around for some time sleep on the patio at night.

While the homeless can blend in with the beach bums at Ocean Beach, it's in the early-morning hours, just after sunrise, that their status is revealed. They creep out of the hideaways where they spent the night, some still wrapped in their sleeping bags. They stumble down the just-waking streets with their large packs and dogs, asking passersby whether they would buy them a cup of coffee.

Past the pier, where the surf meets the cliffs, three young kids struggled to pack up their gear in the early-morning chill. Still bleary-eyed, they shivered against the strong wind, teeth chattering too hard for steady conversation. It was their first stint at Ocean Beach, and they hadn't expected it to be so cold.

Even coming in off the cliffs and into the warmth of the sun, twenty-two-year-old Johnny Carrick's nose and cheeks remained bright and wind chapped, as red as his mussed auburn hair. Johnny had only been traveling for about two months when I spoke with him in San Diego, but he had been living on the streets for more than two years before that, since he aged out of foster care in Visalia, slightly north of Los Angeles. Johnny had bounced in and out of foster homes since he was about three weeks old, moving from family to family and sometimes back to his mother for a few months at a time. His mother was unstable and struggled with drugs, he said, but his time in foster care didn't offer much steadiness either. "Growing up and switching homes all the time, going to different schools, it doesn't help you have a steady lifestyle," Johnny said.

"Destiny" had brought Johnny to Ocean Beach. He had bought a one-way bus ticket to Pismo Beach, just wanting to get away, and fell asleep on the bus, waking up when the driver announced that they were in San Diego. In his two months in San Diego, he mostly stayed around the Ocean Beach area. "I think this is one of the best places to be for homeless youth," he said. "There are churches up on Sunset Cliffs that help give us food and shit and clothe us and help us, like, get bus passes so that we can find work and shit."

We had relocated to a small grassy patch near the pier, just before the sand began. The bright sun warmed us from the chill coming in from the ocean, but the wind still whipped around us, gusting through our clothing and making our eyes water. Several other transients lounged here while we chatted, some lying down and others socializing, and the yips and barks of their tiny Chihuahua-esque dogs were getting lost in the wind. Jonny "Indigenous" Hurst rolled up on a bicycle after some time and joined us, and he played some blues on a beat-up guitar.

The entire time I spoke with Johnny, I felt my eyes wandering over to another kid from his camp. The kid wasn't doing much, just sitting and listening to Johnny speak, but I couldn't look away. While Johnny and his other compatriot bore the dirt-covered, grizzled sort of look of so many street kids, making it impossible to tell whether they were eighteen or forty-eight, this other kid still had the delicate and androgynous features of a child. With thin, fragile limbs tucked in an oversize knit sweater and light blond hair buzzed closed to the skull, this kid couldn't be older than twelve, I thought. "I get that a lot," Shay Ward said. "I'm sixteen."

Shay is a transgender boy who arrived in San Diego about a month after Johnny. Although sixteen is better than twelve, his youth stood in sharp contrast with the men he accompanied. Johnny droned and rambled, freely letting his thoughts and opinions be known and even his conspiracy theories about the Illuminati, while Shay still spoke in the shy one-word answers of a child, divulging the barest minimum only with some prodding. I dragged out of him that he was from Lebanon, Missouri, that his upbringing had been "like any childhood, you know, pretty normal." He explained that when his father had died about three months prior, "I wanted to get out of my hometown, go somewhere new."

I asked where his mother was in all this. "Oh, that's my mom over there," he said, pointing to a bundle of blankets a few feet away, tucked next to the form of a sleeping man. A stout brunette woman startled awake when Shay called out, and sat up, shivering and half-asleep.

Her name is Edie, and at forty-one, she wouldn't consider herself a kid anymore. While this was Shay's first time on the streets, this was not Edie's first experience with homelessness. She knew they'd be on the streets when they left Missouri—she didn't have a job lined up or any extra cash—but after her husband died, "I just wanted to start anew, start fresh," she said. "There were just so many memories there."

She claimed the move had been purely for a fresh start, but more seemed to be at play here than she was willing to let on. She and Shay left for San Diego with a twenty-seven-year-old family friend with whom Edie was romantically involved—the third kid who spent the night with Johnny and Shay on the cliffs—but they had "grown apart," she said, and she was now with Mike, the surly-looking man who slept next to her and was at least a decade her junior. A heavy stutter punctuated her Southern drawl, and her teeth were mangled in a way that suggested heavy drug use. After some prodding, she admitted that she had been addicted to heroin, cocaine, and methadone for several years. "I was actually lucky that my oldest ended up normal, that's how bad

I was on it," she said. "It's not something that I'm proud of. The only thing I do now is weed."

At the very least, Edie seemed to be working through some past traumas. She had had a difficult childhood with a mother who was "a whore, a drunk," and a father who had died young. Her first stint with homelessness began at nineteen—her boyfriend had kicked her out—but eventually she found her husband, who got her sober. Though Edie mourned her husband's death, she later admitted that he was abusive and a philanderer. "I mean, he might have done his wrongs by me, but nobody can actually say that I did not stay with that man until the day he died," she said proudly.

Mike snorted. "Divorce is there for a reason," he said.

"I wasn't raised that way," she retorted, a defensiveness edging into her drawl. "When you marry somebody, it's for forever. It's not, 'Oh, we just got in a spat and it's done.' That's a lot of how it is nowadays."

Edie had the sass of a Southern woman, and she gave me the impression that she was not the sort of person I'd want to mess with, yet there was also something childlike in her demeanor, in the almost immature melodramatic way she spoke of her life and explained her line of thinking. When I looked up her Facebook page, I found her wall littered with the song lyrics, memes, and brassy quotes of a girl much younger than she was, posted with the frequency of a teenager: "I try to make people feel loved and wanted because I know what it's like to not feel loved and wanted." "Raise your hand if you have been acting like you are all okay but inside really you are not." "My spirit animal is 'I Don't Fucking Care Bear.'" Months after we met, she was still posting love notes and tagging her deceased abusive husband: "I am missing you today. I know you are in Heaven but I miss you so much." "'He's gone,' they said. And in that moment my heart shattered into a million pieces and my whole world turned black."

Her page looked like Shay's page: "No I'm not picking my nose, I'm adjusting my piercing." "Fuck all y'all except a select few." "I don't want a lukewarm love. I want it to burn my lips and engulf my soul." Edie tagged Shay often in her posts, in the way friends tag their friends when they see a meme they like: "Yes, I gave you life . . . but really, you gave me mine."

"Being here has made me a stronger woman, even though I'm out on the streets," Edie told me. "I don't like being out on the streets, but it's made me realize that sometimes you've got to start low and build yourself back up, to the person that you want to be."

When I asked how a sixteen-year-old kid factored into her decision to go homeless, she said it was only at Shay's urging that she upended their lives and moved them 1,700 miles away from all they knew. Shay confirmed this, and seemed unmoved by the fact that this decision also meant imminent homelessness. He seemed to take pride in his status—his Facebook URL included the identifier of "dirty kid."

"It'd be nice to have a house," he said. "And one day I'll be in a house. You just got to think positive."

~

Haze's return to California feels like the scene in *The Wizard of Oz* where Dorothy opens the door to a full-color world. In going over his life story, Haze described the first ten years of his life as if he were looking at each moment through a screen window—bits and pieces make their way through, but the big parts remain mostly fuzzy. The events he lived through before he and his mother were reunited are little more than boiled-down plot points, described in a vague, sweeping manner with a few specific details seeping out with some prodding. But Haze could rattle off the specifics of his order at the In-N-Out Mindi took him to after picking him up at the airport (a Triple Triple burger with Animal Style fries and a strawberry shake) and recall the most arbitrary of anecdotes with such abundant detail that I struggled to keep up in my notes. He readily volunteered up minutia such as him and Mindi smoking weed together on that first In-N-Out trip after his return, and him trying to sneak a cigarette from her pack lying on the car's center console—"You could have just asked," Haze remembered Mindi chiding him—yet he was unsure about the dates and his age and other pieces of pertinent information.

Haze will never say a bad word about his mother, or her parenting. Even with the unpredictability of having a drug addict as a mother, he remains loyal to her and she to him. "She's the only person who ever tried to support me," he said. This familial loyalty goes both ways. Even after Haze was convicted of brutally murdering two strangers, Mindi's devotion to her son never wavered. "My son has a good heart," she said. "He is a good person. But when drugs and alcohol are involved, we can all make bad choices and we all become people we really aren't."

It's without a doubt that Mindi truly loves her kids and her family more than anything. But Mindi today is an entirely different person than she was during Haze's childhood, when she was in the throes of drug addiction. Today, after almost five years of sobriety, she is a striking, sturdy woman with thick brunette hair and an open face. She has the look of someone who could take a punch, and has taken her fair share from life, but who would also take you into her arms and comfort you if you were hurt. She was reluctant to talk at first, her answers terse and opaque, as if she were wary of betraying her son even after he had given her permission to speak on his behalf. But she warmed up within minutes, freely doling out the bits of wisdom she picked up on her journey to sobriety.

Mindi was born in Oregon, and just like Haze, her early years were spent on the road. "My dad would kind of go where the work was, and a lot of that was Arizona, Nevada, and sometimes like Utah, or Oregon, California, Washington," she said. "I called it the family tour, the West Coast Tour. The Grateful Dead played at many of those spots, and that's kind of what my parents were doing. My dad would go for the work and my mom was into crafts."

Like her son, she won't say a bad word against her parents. Her parents abused drugs and alcohol heavily in her early years, though her father has been sober now for fifteen years. She was born addicted to heroin and brought up "in an environment where drugs and alcohol were around at all times." These past five years of sobriety, she said, have been the longest she's gone in her entire life without being on any kind of substance.

"It was just a normal thing for me," she said. "When I was a small child, I knew if I didn't feel good, my mother would give me whiskey. I knew I could get that. I didn't realize for many, many years that the world wasn't like that, that everybody wasn't like that."

When her parents broke up, she and her mother moved to live permanently in Oregon. Then her mother got sick, and Mindi began leaning on the crutch that had always been there to support her: "heroin, pills, and meth," she said. For young girls in particular, drug use and sex—and trading sex for drugs—are closely tied, and Mindi was no exception. At thirteen, around the same time her mother passed away, Mindi gave birth to twin girls, born addicted just as she was, whom she gave up for adoption.

She moved to San Francisco with Haze's father shortly after graduating from high school, and at nineteen, she got pregnant with Haze. Although Haze's attorney stated at his sentencing that Haze had been exposed to drugs while in the womb, Mindi asserted that she stayed clean through her pregnancy. "I didn't even do sugar," she said. "After the girls were born and they were given up for adoption, I promised myself that if I was ever blessed to be pregnant again, I would do it right. I didn't even eat meat then."

Haze always stands by his mother, and when I asked him about this discrepancy, he didn't act any differently. "He was just doing it for the court," he said about his attorney's claim. But he slipped up once, saying flat out, "I was born addicted to drugs," and when I reminded him that his mother had said otherwise, he quickly backtracked. "Whether I was actually on drugs or not, it is a chemical dependency that everybody in my family has," he said, stepping over each word with care.

His childhood also didn't completely match Mindi's recollections. Mindi said she was only smoking weed when Haze was a kid, but Haze's memories of car crashes and abusive boyfriends hinted at much harder drug use. Her telling of the accidental dosing when Haze was a toddler didn't mesh either, with her account making her seem less negligent. "He blew his nose on a wet Tampax that had acid on it and accidentally got high," she said. Haze smirked when he heard this. "Is that what she said happened?" he asked.

Haze had one very specific memory from his time in San Diego that seemed to be emblematic of his relationship with his mother—the "only time" he was caught shoplifting, he said. "Nika and Alex"—Mindi's boyfriend's kids, whom he referred to as his stepsiblings—"wanted candy and kept bothering me to get them some, so I went to a Vons," he said. "I was super high and didn't have anyone to cause a distraction, so I just stuffed a bag of Halloween candy down my pants."

When the police arrived, he had stuck by the one lesson his mom was always telling him: keep your mouth shut. The responding officer asked him for his name, his mother's name, his mother's phone number—but he stayed quiet.

"They start bringing me over to the car, and Nika is freaking out, crying," he said. "I'm in the car, like, 'Nika. Shut up.' And the cop is just like, 'Hey there. Is that your brother? Do you know your mom's name? What's your mom's phone number?'"

The officer called Mindi, and Haze could hear her fury through the phone: "What the fuck did he do?" The Vons where Haze was caught wasn't far from the apartment they shared at the time, and from a distance, he could see his mother, "marching across the field, looking like she's about to kick my ass."

"Is this your son, ma'am?" the officer asked. "She said yeah, and started cursing at me," Haze said. The officer thought that, like any parent, Mindi was about to rain down the fear of God on her son for shoplifting. Instead, after cursing at Haze and giving him a slap on the back of the head, "She was like, 'What the hell are you doing getting caught?'" Haze said, doubling over with laughter.

He said that, later, the officer had told his mother that he had caused more problems than some of the officer's thirty-three-year-old parolees. "Walking back to the apartment, Mom was like, 'You didn't say anything, did you? Good kid. Nika, don't snitch on your brother.'"

Mindi chuckled when I asked about this incident. "It was stupid," she said. "It was literally just some candy he shoved down the front of his pants." While she claims that the police didn't call her and that Nika never snitched on her brother—a neighborhood kid had seen it all happening and ran and got her—she doesn't dispute Haze's telling. "The police officer was like, 'You got a real problem with this one, he acts like a thirty-year-old parolee already,' and I was like, 'Oh OK well are you releasing them?'"

Mindi and Haze are cut from the same cloth, but it is uncertain how much of that is the influence of a mother on her child. They have a very specific way of speaking about their family. They will be honest and open about drug use and abuse and neglect, but when it involves somebody they love, they speak about it in a way that completely absolves that person of wrongdoing. It's without question that Mindi's drug addiction affected Haze's life, just like her parents' addiction affected her life, yet they hedge at saying so outright. They lay out the facts of their lives as if recounting the plotline of an uninteresting but detailed movie, speaking about their life as if it didn't happen to them. In this family, loyalty and "no snitching" seem to go beyond the childhood lessons passed on from Mindi to Haze—it's ingrained in their DNA, just one of many familial traits that Mindi and Haze believe to be part of their bloodline: an inclination toward addiction and substance abuse, wanderlust, and a quickness to anger. It's the question of nature versus nurture all over again, unfolding over various generations.

Mindi doesn't try to sugarcoat her mistakes, or her past addictions, but she gets defensive when it comes to her parenting. She'll admit that addiction ruled entire chunks of her life, but she is adamant that she taught Haze the difference between right and wrong and that at his core, he is good. She made a point to say that her other son, Haze's younger half brother, and the other kids she took care of throughout her life turned out all right. "They're members of society," she said. "They have jobs. They have families. They're good people." She wouldn't say it outright, but her message was clear: even with Haze in prison, even if he had been convicted of killing two people, she was a good mother. She had done her best. "Every time he got in trouble and went to juvenile hall, the judge would ask him, 'Do you know right from wrong? Who taught you that?' And he'd say, 'My mom,'" she said.

"I've always had a saying: you can give a kid a book, but you can't make him learn."

~

Near the cliffs where I found Shay and Johnny, rocks jut into the water, creating little nooks and secret hideaways along the coast. Families scramble over these boulders throughout the day, exploring the small private sanctuaries that appear when the waves are docile. But come high tide, the ocean swallows up the rocks once again, and with them, the ghosts of the kids who were once there, the kids who painstakingly scratched their existence onto those rocks. Years of graffiti cover the rocks, calcified into permanence over time. Infinity signs, hearts, sunbursts, and stick figures; A + L, Tay + Mal, Alyssa + Brenner, Camila 9/21/11. "Drink Fight Fuck," one message reads. "Zeos was here," states another.

One rock bears a crude carving of a crown, big and jagged like one worn by a cartoon king. In the center, an *O* and a *B* intertwine. Few who remain at Ocean Beach today are familiar with this symbol. But for Haze, it was the sign of his people: the Ocean Beach Krowners.

The very first tattoo he got—a stick-and-poke tattoo that he said he did himself when he was eleven—is an homage to the Krowners, a jagged "OBK" over his heart. Like Haze, the majority of his Krowner friends were street kids, runaways, youthful miscreants with nowhere to go. Some had homes and families to return to at the end of the day. Many did not. They weren't a gang in the way most criminal street gangs operate, but they were friends, a crew, and they had each other's backs, no matter what. Together, they escaped the abuse and pain of their pasts with psychedelics and alcohol, heroin and meth, and spent their days skateboarding, surfing, smoking, selling drugs, and having sex with "beach girls." "Beach girls love lost teenage boys," Haze said.

"Sex, drugs, and skateboard gangs," Haze said. "All-day parties. My days on Ocean Beach were the funnest times of my young years."

Mindi freely admits that she lost control of Haze during their San Diego period. Haze was never the same again after Virginia, she said, even though she claimed to not know exactly what he went through there. "His father was kind of unstable mentally, and when he and I were together, he wouldn't necessarily physically abuse me, but he would mentally abuse me. I knew he probably did the same type of thing to Haze," she said. She said she tried repeatedly to get in contact with Haze over the three years he lived in Virginia, but couldn't—Haze's father and grandmother wouldn't allow it. Haze's grandmother maintained that she never saw any instance of abuse between Haze's father and Mindi. She also said that Haze was always allowed to call and talk to Mindi, and that his father even brought him to visit Mindi's parents in Oregon.

During this time, Mindi also lost custody of Haze's younger half brother and started using drugs again to cope with not having her children with her. "If he was allowed to just stay with me, and his grandmother never took him from me, everything would have been completely different," she said. "That's really when things started going bad for Haze."

Haze believed for a while what he said his grandmother and father told him—that his mother had abandoned him and voluntarily sent him to live with his father—and that resentment drove him to act aloof and cold toward her when they were first reunited. And to Mindi, when he returned, his time in Virginia had changed him enough that he was unrecognizable to her, no longer the "happy kid" who "was very smart, loved to joke, and loved to tell stories."

"He was so set in acting out that it was really hard," she said. "He was open with me about what he was doing, but at that point, he just did what he thought he could get away with or do."

When she was reunited with Haze, Mindi had to keep it together enough to care not just for him, but for her boyfriend's two young children—Nika and Alex. She continued using drugs, she said, but in a way that was manageable. "I was what they called a functioning addict," she said. "I did methadone in my red beer. I didn't want to do pills and I didn't want to do heroin. I was able to volunteer at the kids' schools and I was really involved in their educations.

"But Haze, by then, was in middle school, and he was just making bad choices."

Haze joined up with the Ocean Beach Krowners not long after his return from Virginia. He was at Ocean Beach one day when he met the kid he knew only as Smiley, who eventually brought him into the fold. "We were just best friends from the first," Haze said. "We both had drug addicts for moms. It was like, 'Hi. I know you.'"

Few in the group knew each other's actual names, but they were a family in a way that they all craved but did not know that they needed. The crew ran rampant through San Diego and its surrounding towns, robbing people and local shops, and then exchanging the stolen goods for money or drugs back at the beach. They had a system: several of them would enter a store at different times. One of them would create a distraction, while the other one ran off with the booty. In one instance, Haze said he went into a grocery store in Lakeside and filled a cart with cake, ice cream, carne asada, charcoal, lighter fluid, and liquor, and then just walked out and hid in a nook of a nearby apartment building and waited for the cops to leave. "We had a two-day barbecue," he said.

Through all this, Haze still continued to abuse drugs heavily, trying everything from psychedelics to heroin. He skipped school and ran away on a regular basis, getting in trouble everywhere he turned. While attending Tierra del Sol Middle School, he got drunk and mooned his classmates during an assembly. He got caught with pot at school, another time with porn. A neighbor once reported him for assaulting his mother, which he said was a misunderstanding—he didn't want to go to school, and when his mother was dragging him down the stairs, he slipped and his foot hit her left shoulder, he said.

Mindi tried with him, but a kid like Haze at this age would have been a challenge for even a fully functioning parent with time and resources. They had an understanding that he would be open with her about what he was doing. "I would have these nightmares that the kids he hung out with wouldn't know what to do and I would find him at the bottom of our steps, dead," Mindi said. "I knew what he was doing, that was when he got into heroin and meth, and I just knew, through my experience, if you don't know what to do in a situation like that, people end up dead. They end up scared."

His stepsister at the time, Nika, was four or five years younger than him, and only six years old when he came into her life. She remembers going with Mindi and her brother, Alex, to visit him in juvenile hall and that "he was always getting into trouble." One night, he stole her dad's car and crashed it, she said.

Nika has pleasant memories of her time with Mindi—"She was a wonderful mother," Nika said—but she blanked out much of her time with Haze. He scared her. Beyond the trouble he caused for his family, he would do odd things like cut his hand to swap blood with his friends. When she was eight, he came home and told her that he was the devil.

"He told me he was the devil and I sold my soul to him," she said. "He wrote up a contract and everything."

He manipulated her into signing it, she said. And then, as the "owner" of her soul, he began to molest her—just as in Virginia, he directed his pain and anger into hurting other children. Though Haze and Mindi deny these allegations, Nika began on a downward spiral not long after her time with Haze. She became addicted to drugs and was homeless—her spiral reflected what Haze experienced, to some point.

Mindi, who still stays in touch with Nika and her father, worried that Nika may have conflated some drug-induced delusions with her memories of Haze. But it's worth noting that what Nika told me Haze made her do was what Haze told me the daughter of Mindi's abusive boyfriend did to him when he was still a child—children exposed to complex trauma may attempt to communicate their traumatic past in a reenactment in their day-to-day behavior, according to the National Child Traumatic Stress Network. No matter what happened, to this day, Nika struggles with the consequences. Perhaps, in a way, Haze does too.

~

It took Mindi getting arrested on drug-related charges in order for her to get clean. Now with the benefit of hindsight, she can look back on both her life and Haze's life and can see the deep impact their drug use had on their actions. "We all have choices to make, and when you make bad choices, certain things happen," she said. "But when you're on drugs, you don't see a choice, other than maintaining your addiction. You get caught in a cycle of maintaining your addiction and doing whatever you think you need to do to maintain that."

Juvenile court sent Haze to a boys' group home in El Centro when he was thirteen. He doesn't have many memories from his time there, which he blamed on being heavily medicated ("Trazodone, Zoloft, Seroquel, Risperdal," he said; "I was a zombie")—but he remembered all the good times he had when he would return to San Diego on a home pass for the weekend. Even though his mother was living out of a car, they used a friend's address to allow for home visitations. And then he'd just run wild around Ocean Beach. According to Haze, his best friend, Smiley, had been shot and killed just the year before he left for the group home, but the dirty kid network at Ocean Beach endured. He never wanted for company when he was at Ocean Beach.

Haze knew he couldn't smoke weed because they would run a drug test on him when he got back, but his first weekend in Ocean Beach, he accidentally ate some Starbursts that were laced with LSD. "I was like, oh crap. They're going to drug-test me. I saw my mom on the pier, and I ran over to her. 'Hey Mom, they can't drug-test you for LSD, right?' She said no, that they'd have to do a spinal tap in order to do that. I asked whether she'd ever consent to one being done on me, and she said, 'Hell no.'" That first weekend, he and a friend paddled out some surfboards and sat in the waves as the high rolled in. With each visit after that, he said, he'd return to the group home, still tripping and with cigarettes taped to the inside of his thigh.

When he was fifteen, he got out of the group home and had nowhere to go. Eager to get off the streets, Mindi returned to Oregon to live with her father. She claims that Haze's social worker was aware of this and told her the court would still release him into her custody if she moved, but when the time came, the judge refused to do so. Reluctantly, Mindi reached out to Haze's paternal grandmother for help—she had worked for the state of Washington and allegedly had connections—and she arranged for Haze to live with his father in Washington. Haze didn't want to go anywhere near the man he said had molested him, but he had no choice. "I just wanted out of California," Haze said. "They would have kept me incarcerated until my eighteenth birthday." He was supposed to stay with his father until he was eighteen, but less than a year later, he was back with his mother, her new boyfriend, and his grandfather in Oregon.

His grandfather was sober at this point, and he had little tolerance for the rest of his family who continued to use. Mindi readily admitted to heavily using again—her stepmother of years had died, and her death had reopened old wounds from when Mindi's own mother had passed years before. "I started doing heroin and meth again," she said. "I didn't want to be around my dad, who was clean. He was like, 'You can't do drugs here, and if you're going to do that, you're not welcome here.' And then Haze ended up stealing from my dad so Haze wasn't welcome in my dad's home either."

Soon, they were out on the streets again, sleeping with dozens of other vagrants under the Hawthorne Bridge and the Morrison Bridge along the Willamette River in Portland, and under an overpass on Fourth Avenue in Spokane. Haze started wandering away from his mother during this time and becoming more independent. At seventeen, he took to the road, and his travels as a dirty kid drifter began. Before he knew it, he was on to the next great adventure, on the road, hitchhiking and riding freight trains across the country.

Haze's happy, drug-fueled days at Ocean Beach ended with him in the damp chill of the Pacific Northwest, on the streets with his mother and her new boyfriend. Summer must come to an end sometime, even in the land of endless summer. But he'd be back. And it was here, at Ocean Beach, that he'd find Lila Alligood, setting in motion the final domino on the path to murder.

SEVEN

The Phases of the Moon

Lila went by the name Māhealani, a name Haze said she got while living on the Big Island in Hawaii, where she'd spent part of her life. It means "the phases of the moon," Haze said, but other definitions include "bright moonlight" or "heavenly moonlight." Haze sometimes called her Māhea for short, but he rarely referred to her as Lila, her given name. In prison, he wears a cross-stitch necklace around his neck that he made himself: M + H.

One of the first lies I caught Haze in was about this young woman he still calls the love of his life, even after all these years of separation. In Marin County Jail, he spun a mournful tale of how they met. He had waded into the ocean at the off-leash dog area of Ocean Beach with weights tied to his wrists and ankles, ready to die and end it all. It was dusk, and the waves inky black, but still, Lila jumped in after him and pulled him back to the shore. "I was half-drowned," he said, "and I thought she was an angel."

Later, in the prison visiting room in Corcoran, he said he met her upon his return to San Diego, after several years of hitchhiking and train hopping around the country, hanging with the Rainbows and the activists with the Occupy movement in San Francisco and Oakland. It was the summer of 2013, just after his twenty-first birthday and Lila's sixteenth. "I was like, who is this heroin-addicted chick?" Haze laughed.

"She was bouncing back and forth from her mom's house to the street, getting high, and kicking it with all my friends," he said. "Everyone was like, 'Watch out, she's thirteen, she's thirteen.' But she had a boyfriend then, who was my age. And I was like, no way. She's drinking and doing drugs with the best of us."

After I called him out on his two different versions of their first meeting, he backtracked and said while the story of her saving him from a suicide attempt wasn't how they met, she did stop him from walking out into the ocean that first night, completely by chance. After they had sex in a public restroom at Ocean Beach—he knows they had sex but they had taken so many drugs by then that he can't remember it—he left her at a little beach squat he had set up and he headed toward the ocean.

"I was going to do it," he insisted. "I was just going to wade out to the water and let it happen, but then she came and got me and said, 'Hey, let's go get high.'"

A few nights later, he caught her with a needle in her arm, trying to overdose on heroin. "We saved each other," Haze said. "The truth of it is that both of us were pretty much ready to end it that very day on the beach, and we just stumbled into each other."

Haze spoke of Lila in absolutes. They were kindred spirits, and she was the love of his life, the only person with whom he would be willing to live out the rest of his days. But in the hours of conversation we had about her, his memories reflected little of her personality or what it was that Haze loved about her. His stories about her were mostly about her drug use and the drug-fueled sex they had. Whenever there's a romantic relationship at the center of a murder case, people always imagine some sort of Bonnie and Clyde ride-or-die situation. His dedication to her fits that trope, but not much else does. When he spoke of their relationship, it felt generic, like when middle school tweens write moody song lyrics on their arms—you never believe that they actually feel that way or can comprehend what those lyrics are saying, but they identify with them all the same because that's what they think they're supposed to be doing when it comes to romantic love. It felt like Haze was just saying what he thought one would say about the supposed love of one's life.

Investigators believe that Lila first met Haze when she was twelve, but Haze said they didn't get together romantically until that summer of 2013. She had been hanging around the street kids at Ocean Beach for some time and dabbling in hard drugs. Her supplier was supposedly a friend of her family, Haze said, and her mother had asked him to look out for her. When he had to leave town on an errand, he turned to Haze to take over his duties.

"He asked me to babysit her, and I was like, what?" Haze said. "And he said, just sit on her, man. Don't let her go anywhere. And I was like, 'OK, give me your drugs.' And he gave me his crystal meth, heroin, syringes. And I was like, 'Give me some cash too.' And he gave me four or five hundred dollars."

Haze was almost giddy recollecting their first week together. "She was so funny," he said. "I said, 'Hey, I'm supposed to babysit you.' And she was all drugged out and was like, 'No, I don't need a baby.' And I said, 'No, I need to stick with you. We're attached at the hip.' And she just kind of like looked at her hip and was like, 'Whaaaa?' and I had to be like, 'No, not literally.' She said, 'Well, do you have any drugs?' And I was like, 'Okay, let's go.'"

He chuckled. "We both got so high that first night."

That first week, Lila balked at having a babysitter, albeit one that had sex with her and gave her drugs. They spent the week doing what they usually did, getting drunk and partying on the beach, and she'd try to sneak away whenever his head was turned. But he'd always find her. And before they knew it, they were inseparable.

One afternoon in the prison visiting room, Haze took a sip from the kiwi strawberry Snapple that I had bought him from one of the visiting-room vending machines and smiled. "Māhealani was crazy about everything kiwi strawberry," he said.

His dedication to Lila was baffling. According to him, he has never lacked for romantic companionship. He said he had been having casual sex with girls since before he even hit puberty—he began in Virginia with some neighborhood kids because that was what they thought they were supposed to do. He said he became a father at age twelve—twins, Johnny and Crystal, who died two months after they were born. But come the summer of 2013, he found the one person he could not be without.

When I asked him what made him stick with Lila over all the other girls he'd met in his travels, he looked at me as if I'd eaten paste. "I fell in love with her," he said. He said it with the conviction of a man telling an idiot that the earth is round and the sky is blue. But what is love to a kid like Haze, a kid who has only experienced hurt and more hurt, inadvertent or otherwise, from the ones tasked with loving and caring for him unconditionally? What is love to a kid who only understands three emotions—happiness, anger, and sadness? What is love to a kid who has probably never even met a couple in a healthy, loving relationship?

To him, love means never being apart. Never being without the other. It means never saying no because, Lord knows, he could never say no to his Māhealani. It means recognizing all that has been shattered and destroyed and left to fester and rot inside you, and still sticking around, knowing full well that you won't be able to fix it.

"Anyone who is any kind of falling apart has a broken child inside them, and they always will," Haze said. "Two people who have that and see that and accept that broken piece of you and still love you, no matter what? That was us."

Love doesn't mean no more pain or no more worry. Lila had at least six miscarriages in the two years they were together, Haze said, and the last one nearly killed her. Love doesn't mean no more drugs, because as long as there was still pain, there needed to be drugs to numb it.

Love doesn't even mean that you don't hurt each other, because Lord knows, they hurt each other. Even in the best of circumstances on the streets, Haze and Lila both could be irritable and impatient, exhausted and cold and sick of sleeping outdoors. Especially coming down from a high, they would nitpick and squabble like any other couple, over little things like someone hogging the blanket. But for Haze and Lila, their disagreements also got physical. To them, love means punches, fistfights, causing actual damage to the other person. "It was kind of like foreplay," Haze smirked.

Haze shrugged off questions about what it was about Lila that drew him to her, what it was about her that made him love her. At first, he said it was her "don't give a fuck" attitude, but it took several more conversations for him to fully open up about it.

"It's really, really wrong," Haze said. "But the perfect person for me is a younger, crazier version of my mother, and that's what Māhealani is. Strawberry blonde, a redhead in the sun. My little brother does the same thing. We date women who remind us of our mother. And my mother has dated men who were me in the future."

But it wasn't just the physical resemblance. Lila and Mindi were made of the same stuff, Haze said. They were both survivors, fighters, women who went through hell but still came out standing on the other side. They were "hard-core, put together even though they're falling apart . . . That's the biggest thing right there," he said. "They could be falling into a million pieces and still be able to keep themselves and others together." They kept him together, even in the midst of drug addiction. In a way, Haze admitted later, his and Lila's dependency on drugs meant they had to be dependent on each other. For Haze and Lila, love was less a fairy tale and more about attaching your broken self to another broken person. They were two jagged, banged-up pieces of a puzzle, shoved together by life. It may not have been a perfect fit, but if you smash any two pieces together with enough force, they kind of form a whole.

Lila has never spoken publicly about her relationship with Haze. She did not respond to any of my inquiries. But after the sentencing, her attorney painted a very different portrait of her client, one in which Lila was an impressionable young girl manipulated by drugs and an older man.

"It was the drugs and the love she had for Mr. Lampley," said her attorney, Amy Morton. "It was a very twisted type of companionship. They were both people who had holes in their hearts, and when they met each other, they got involved in heavy drugs."

Lila and her family have declined to reveal much about her background, but according to those who knew her, she spent much of her life bouncing between Hawaii and Southern California, attending second grade in Santa Barbara and some high school on the Big Island. Her Facebook page is a mishmash of smiling selfies and beach photos, shaka signs in front of lush vegetation, and funny faces with friends in classrooms. She had fun with different hairstyles through the years, wearing it long and dark in some photos and maroon and multicolored in others, before ultimately going short and blonde. In her last post—August 29, 2015, just over a month before the killings—her shoulder-length hair is big and wild, kissed by the sun. She is smiling brightly under a light smattering of freckles, and appears to be sitting in the front seat of a car. "Spend a day surfing," she wrote. "I promise you'll feel better."

She posted in June 2013 that she was "glad to finally be back in California," which matches Haze's recollection of when they first got together romantically. But how, when, and why she got involved with the street kids and began abusing drugs remains a mystery.

Lila cried throughout much of the criminal proceedings, and at her sentencing, she was the only one of the three to read her statement to the victims' families herself. "Of the three, I sensed the most humanity in her," Lokita Carter, Steve's widow, wrote on her blog. But the detectives who put her behind bars were more skeptical.

"I think it was more for show than it was genuine," said one investigator. "We did this investigation for months, and the phone calls and letters she would write and stuff, there was just no remorse." She was particularly callous in bragging about the killings to her cellmate, Pamela Bullock. According to the cellmate, she referred to Audrey Carey as "the bitch," and when the talk came to Steve Carter, she said, "The old man needed to die."

"Haze was more street-smart, but she is a very smart individual," the investigator said. "She's very articulate and very smart. I think she could have been a straight-A student if she had wanted to be."

The investigator added: "She ran that relationship. Just reading their letters to each other, she was a mother figure to him. She was always correcting him—you did this wrong, you did that wrong."

Investigators fingered Haze as the ringleader, but believed Lila to be manipulating him behind the scenes. According to a former school friend, this sort of behavior would not be out of character for Lila. "Lila kind of always had this attitude that the world owed her something," said the friend, who asked to be identified only as Kay. "She just seemed really unhappy, but it wasn't just that she never had enough—it wasn't OK for other people to have what she didn't have."

The Lila she knew took teenage drama to a whole new level, Kay said. She spread cruel rumors, turned friends against one another, and went out of her way to always appear to be the victim. "Rumors and stuff like that, a lot of girls participate in that," Kay said. "The spreading of rumors wasn't the problem. It was the viciousness of the rumors, not just about me but about other people, and how intense she was on not just spreading them, but making sure everyone hated the people the rumors were about."

Kay said that she and Lila became friends their sophomore year at Parker School, a prestigious private school in Waimea. Others had warned Kay against Lila, but "she was just very funny and seemed to be happy all the time," Kay said. "She was very sarcastic and jokey, which I am too, so it was pretty easy to get along." They did normal high school girl things, going to Starbucks and smoking weed and hanging out and riding bikes around the island. She remembered her being very smart, but inconsistent when it came to her schoolwork.

During this time, Kay became close with Lila's mother and younger sister—Lila's mother and father got divorced early in Lila's life, Kay said, and while Lila was open about everything involving her mother and her sister, she would clam up when it came to talking about her dad. They lived in high-end luxury apartments, and all in all, Lila seemed to have a fairly typical, upper-middle-class island upbringing, Kay said.

"Lila was pretty normal up until she went to California during our sophomore summer," Kay said. "She went to art school there, I guess. She said she smoked a lot of weed and some other stuff, but she had always been a stoner before that . . . She had really long hair that she loved and she had dreaded it when she was in California. Before she came back, she had buzzed it all off. That was really out of character for her. She talked about this guy she met while she was in art school who was older, but she never really gave us the details of all the stuff that she had done and the people that she met."

Lila acted out quite a bit, and things only got worse after that summer. Kay got the impression that her mother didn't know how to rein her in. She got expelled from Parker School after she was arrested trying to steal alcohol from a local grocery store, Kay said. She transferred to Honoka'a High School, and soon was arrested for trying to sell weed on campus. Her mother wanted to move the whole family back to Southern California for a fresh start, and the night before the move, Lila ran away, Kay said.

Lila also had a hypersexuality about her that, looking back now, feels alarming, Kay said. She told everyone that a girl in their class had tried to touch her at a campout, but later, when Kay pressed for more information, she explained that that had never happened at all. She fixated on boys and wanting boys to want her back. Just before their friendship ended, Lila told Kay that she wanted them "to be the kind of friends who could practice kissing," Kay said. Shortly after Kay said she wasn't comfortable with that, Lila spread a sexually explicit rumor about Kay that was so heinous that Kay feels uncomfortable even discussing it now. "Part of me thinks it's because I told her I wasn't interested in having a friendship like that," Kay said. "That's why she went out and took control of the situation."

While Haze didn't say much about Lila's personality or the dynamics of their relationship, he scoffed at the idea that he had corrupted her innocence in some way. "If she wasn't on a dark and demented path when we met," he said, "then I don't know what dark and demented is."

According to Haze, her father was "a major meth cook and beat her up until the age of four." Public criminal records show that he had a history of driving under the influence and public intoxication, dating back to before Lila was born, but nothing indicating that he had ever been arrested for manufacturing drugs. Her mother fled with her and her younger sister to Southern California, but she still returned to Hawaii on a regular basis. She got her driver's license in Hawaii, the only one of the three to have one, Haze said. She turned to drugs at a young age for the same reason Haze did—to numb the pain and trauma. She learned to drive, Haze said, while high on heroin.

They wrote each other in county jail until the sheriff's department put a stop to it, but Haze said they still found a way to communicate. When she became a laundry worker, a responsibility only granted to inmates on good behavior, he had people tuck messages into the corner of the mesh laundry bags for her to find. He had "homeboys" make her cards and send them to her from the outside.

Haze doesn't doubt that she loved him just as much as he loved her. He believed for a while that the tears she shed in court were for him— for each time she heard his name. At the preliminary hearing, Sergeant Scott Buer with the Marin County Sheriff's Department testified that the former cellmate in county jail said that Lila had asked her to print out and send her some photos of Haze from Facebook when she was released from custody.

A few weeks after they got together at Ocean Beach, Lila and Haze headed north. While it may be warmer and less rainy in Southern California in the winter season, Northern California is more equipped to care for the homeless when the cold strikes. "You can stay warm in Northern California in the winter," he said. A buddy named David joined them on the trek north, and together, they stole some bicycles and headed up the coast. Outside a 7-Eleven in Oceanside, a couple bought them groceries and Amtrak train tickets to Oakland. The couple gave them money as well, which they spent on pot before they boarded the train. They ended up in Berkeley, where they split off from their friend David and spent the next few months going between Berkeley and San Francisco, where Haze sold drugs. They took a few side trips to Oregon, where Haze met up with his mother and attempted to fulfill his cabin dream. But by then, his grandfather had moved onto the property full-time. According to Haze, his grandfather said there was only enough room for two people on the property—and Haze wasn't going to stay without Lila.

Eventually they headed back south, and at Venice Beach, they ran into the boyfriend of an acquaintance, who had a Jeep. "I'm going east," he told them. "Do you want to go east?"

"We looked at each other for half a second and said, 'Yeah,'" Haze said.

It was Lila's first big trip. Haze said they got onto Interstate 10 and stopped at Quartzsite, Arizona, before heading north to bum around for a few days in Colorado. The Jeep's owner had been talking about signing the car over to them for $2,000, Haze said, but at a rest stop in Nebraska, they heard him talking on the phone about his plan to just string them along and then refuse to give them the car, even though they had already given him $1,500. They waited for him to go take a shower, and then they took the car, with the man's dog still in it. They had to take the dog, Haze said, because the dog really belonged to the man's girlfriend, and he beat it. A woman—the alleged girlfriend—later posted on Haze's Facebook a vague but accusatory comment that didn't quite jibe with Haze's account: "Time to pay for real for taking Bear. I guess you didn't know that was my fucking dog."

From there, it was a whirlwind of crossing state lines, picking up hitchhikers, and partying with the local dirty kids wherever they stopped. For all he had suffered through in life, Haze only had one real fear, and that's driving, a remnant of all the wrecks he experienced during his childhood, as a passenger to drivers under the influence. He relied on Lila to drive the entire way. They hit up Kentucky and New Orleans, but Haze had started dreaming about the cabin in Oregon again. Lila didn't want to leave New Orleans, but she wanted this dream too, Haze said. "She was always talking about how she missed growing pot on her family's farm," he said. So they left New Orleans, stopping in Texas for just long enough to panhandle cash for the ride back. The plan was to stop in San Diego one last time to reunite the dog with the owner, get some marijuana seeds from some people they knew there, and have Lila see her mom one last time before going off the grid. But on their first night back in San Diego, they fell asleep in the car after smoking a blunt. They had parked in a no-parking area, and when the police came, they found Lila and Haze in a vehicle that had been reported stolen.

It was the summer of 2015, just months before the murders. Haze got out of jail fairly quickly, but Lila was still seventeen at this point. Haze had no idea where she was being held or whether she would be released anytime soon. He got it in his head that she was going to be shipped back to Hawaii and he would never see her again. He fell into a desperate tailspin of drugs and alcohol, and started hooking up with another girl, but he posted on Facebook what he believes to essentially be marriage vows for himself and Lila: *Aloha au 'ia 'oe (I love you) / No kêia la, no kea pô, a mau loa (From this day, from this night, forever more)*

/ *Male ana e pili mai aloha kâua (We two will cling to love in marriage)* /
Aloha aku nô, aloha mai nô (I give my love to you, you give your love to me).

And just when he'd lost all hope, he got a response to his post: "Yes." Lila posted on his Facebook page that she was being held at the Las Colinas Detention Facility in San Diego, the detention center for women. Within a few weeks, they would be reunited. And at this point, they weren't taking any more chances. It was time to get to the cabin. It was time to live their dreams. And this time, nothing would stop them.

EIGHT

Haight Street
San Francisco, California

Christian Garmisa-Calinsky sat at a table at Coffee to the People one afternoon, a few years after the killings, nodding and waving at acquaintances as he took care of business on his phone. Dark tattoos cover almost every inch of visible skin on this burly bearded man, including his bespectacled face, yet somehow every time I see him, he's found a new way to add to his embellishments, whether it be glitter or stickers or some other silly thing one of his kids dashed off on him.

Dave in Buena Vista Park in the summer of 2011 may have been my introduction to the world of street kids, but it was meeting Christian that opened my eyes to their reality. The first time I heard him speak, we were packed in a tiny meeting room at the local police station, shortly after Haze's, Lila's, and Sean's faces began appearing across the evening news. In their dazed mug shots, Lila's thick blonde hair was clumped in dreadlocks, her round face covered with meth sores; Sean's blue eyes were glazed over; while Haze held the deranged stare of a deer caught in headlights. They looked unwashed, strung out, and, to the dozens of Upper Haight neighborhood residents who attended the meeting, they looked just like every other young homeless vagrant drawn to these streets.

Hysteria reigned that night, with neighbors spilling forth all the complaints they'd never felt were appropriate to voice before. "It has become a nightmare," said one longtime resident, Kate Lust. "It used to be just a handful of kids that no one really begrudged. But now there's a whole culture they're setting up of people who don't like the other people. They're now on every corner. It smells like a sewer."

These were the same neighbors who'd introduced me to the world of street kids back in 2011 by describing them as "mostly harmless," yet here one man raised the issue of every street kid being armed and dangerous. "My wife won't go into Buena Vista Park because we don't know if they have guns," he said.

"The majority of these people are not armed with firearms," Station Captain John Sanford responded. "Our officers . . . are making contact with these individuals every single day. I do not want this community to be up in arms and scared that every individual out there is armed with guns."

"It only takes one," someone in the middle of the room muttered.

In this claustrophobic space where fear and anger collided, Christian stood against the mob, speaking for the kids he now served—the kid he once was. "You're just picking the garbage from one corner to another," one neighbor said, criticizing the police's enforcement strategy. "Whoa!" Christian shouted. "You're talking about people, not garbage."

Christian told me later that he'd expected this reaction. These days, San Francisco isn't so much in the midst of a Summer of Love as it is deep within a Spring Awakening of Wealth. The gap between the rich and poor continues to grow at an astounding rate. A 2014 report by the city's Human Services Agency found that San Francisco's income inequality is worse than in developing countries like Rwanda and Guatemala. Tech start-ups receive millions in venture capital funding each day, yet the service workers who prepare their catered meals and bus engineers to their sprawling campuses on the Peninsula are sleeping in their cars and working multiple "gig" industry jobs to get by.

The median household income is almost $97,000, more than one and a half times the national median, but teachers, law enforcement, and other municipal employees can no longer afford to live in the city of San Francisco, where, by 2018, the median price of a single-family home hit a jaw-dropping $1.61 million.

When you're traveling down a path paved with gold, the last thing you want to pass is a homeless encampment, a reminder of the stark poverty that still exists outside the tech bubble. Christian knows very well that for far too many in San Francisco, addressing the issue of homelessness is more about figuring out how to make it less of an inconvenience for themselves than figuring out how to help those without homes. The last homeless tally in San Francisco put the count at about 7,500, with about one-third of those individuals being thirty years of age or younger and almost 50 percent being forty years or younger. In 2016, voters passed a ballot measure banning tents on city sidewalks, but failed to pass the ballot measures that would have funded more housing for the homeless—meaning that while voters supported getting the homeless off the streets, they didn't particularly care about where they'd go after that.

And then there are the street kids. What little charity we are willing to give does not seem to extend far enough to reach this particular element of the homeless population. Cicely Hansen was part of the Summer of Love, but as the owner of a vintage clothing store on Haight Street, she's had enough with these kids. "To me, they're not street kids," she said. "They're vagrants who choose not to be part of the culture. They're just hanging around, hoping for free money."

In all fairness, Haight Street can get unruly with all the kids and their drug use. The neighborhood residents have seen their share of bad behavior, especially with the proliferation of more hard-core drugs like opiates, heroin, and crystal meth. But at the heart of the issue is unpredictability. Back in 2011 when I was traipsing through Buena Vista Park, talking to Dave Thompson, one dog walker told me that he never knew what he was going to get from these kids when he encountered them in the parks. Some were "pharmaceutically adjusted," he said, like the time a disoriented man stumbled out of the brush with his pants around his ankles and spooked the dogs. Even when these kids aren't high, though, they're brash and loud, and they take up space in ways we as a society have deemed inappropriate. It's hard to walk down the sidewalk at any time of day without having to navigate around a group or two, often with large dogs and even larger packs in tow, and we hate and fear them because we don't understand them. "I think what people are fearful of are people they don't understand," Christian said. "I think they're especially fearful when a group of people they don't understand gets together."

In the years that I've known Christian, it's been a joy to watch his successes come to fruition. The first time I interviewed him was at Mom's Body Shop, where he did piercings while running his nonprofit, Taking it to the Streets. He quit his piercing job to focus full-time on his work with street kids, setting up shop at Coffee to the People before eventually opening a brick-and-mortar storefront right on Haight Street where the kids could hang out and he and his staff could do their work. He got married, adopted a dog, and moved to Oakland with his family—the San Francisco equivalent of getting a house with a white picket fence in the suburbs. Looking at his life now, it's hard to believe that just ten years ago, he was bouncing between the county jail and Golden Gate Park, constantly strung out and searching for his next hit. "I wasn't doing drugs to get high," he said. "I was trying to kill myself. I was doing drugs to die and for some reason, I couldn't. I'd wake up six hours later and be like, 'Fuck.'"

Christian was born in Oklahoma to an abusive mother who would beat him hard enough to break his bones. He started running away at ten, crashing at the homes of friends and family members until he was fourteen, when he began traveling. He had already been using drugs before he ended up on the streets, and he relied on "a lot of crank because I didn't want to sleep, not on the streets." He landed in San Francisco following a stint in Portland, Oregon, in 1996 and continued to spend his days feeding his drug addiction. "There's just really no end to it until something clicks for you," he explained. "That happened for me in jail."

He had been in and out of jail enough times that the deputies knew him and would bring him treats every once in a while. "I was in the hole, and I woke up and there was a venti Starbucks coffee sitting on my bars," Christian said. "And it was like, 'Fuck, I've got it so good!' I literally said that out loud while I was in the hole in jail because I got some fucking cold coffee on my bars. I snapped. I was like, 'What the hell did I just say?' I actually said it out loud. It was very real to me how good I actually had it, just because I had cold coffee sitting on my jail bars. That changed my whole perspective."

The premise behind his nonprofit was simple: getting housing for homeless youth. To get housing, kids had to clean up Haight Street, picking up garbage and doing quick beautification projects. One stunning example of their work was when they painted the steps at Buena Vista Park purple. The volunteer work in the neighborhood earned them goodwill with the residents and provided the kids with a structure and understanding of responsibility and of holding a steady job. Each kid in his program went through counseling, and he and his team helped them figure out what they wanted to do, whether that meant going back to school or getting a part-time job or exploring a certain talent.

For sure, a lot of these kids needed drug treatment, mental health care, mentorship, education. But first they needed housing, Christian said. Maslow's hierarchy of needs lists shelter as one of the first and most basic requirements for survival, along with clothing, sleep, and food—all items that aren't exactly guaranteed if you're living on the street. As overly simplistic as it seems, it was a start, the first step toward stability for kids who have only known instability.

As we sat chatting at Coffee to the People, a teen walked in and caught Christian's eye. The teen had the same round cherubic face as Lila Alligood. But with clean blonde curls and a sensible knee-length skirt, the teen looked like just that—a teen. Like a kid, fresh with potential.

"You got it?" Christian asked.

"I start tomorrow at 11:30," the teen said proudly. The teen had just gotten a job.

"Hell yeah, look at that!" Christian gave the teen a high five.

"I'll see you later," the teen said. "I'm going to run home."

"Sounds good. Congratulations."

After the teen left, Christian took care to refer to the teen with the pronouns "they" and "their," explaining that the teen was one of five kids born to a mother currently living in Golden Gate Park and had struggled for some time "dealing with gender stuff, dealing with sexuality, dealing with acceptance of themselves."

He spoke excitedly about this family, beaming as he bragged about one brother's progress. "When he first came into the program, one loud noise, he'd be on the ground in the fetal position, shaking for ten minutes," he said. "You'd have to pet him back to life. Now he wears a headset and talks on it and dresses super nice with ties every day. It's a huge fucking change for him, from, like, undiagnosed autism that was severe to being able to function in a high-functioning setting like that. He still has his tics and all that, but he's doing real well at this job."

Christian boasted that he was able to get housing for three of the five kids, all three of whom were also holding steady jobs. The youngest, twelve, however, was too young for the program. She still lived in the park.

~

In one of our conversations, I expressed some frustration to Christian about the fact that the only solutions we have for youth homelessness seem to comprise of just treating the symptom—responding to the crisis only once the kids hit the streets. We don't seem to have a way, I said, to prevent homelessness in the first place.

He shrugged. That's the unfortunate reality we live in, he said. There are far too many reasons why these kids end up on the streets—abuse, trauma, addiction, substance abuse, mental illness, bad parents, a broken foster care system—and there's no way to fix them all, short of hitting a giant "Reset" button on the systems we have in place. "You are never going to fix the foster care system. You are never going to fix what's coming from the top," Christian said. "The city is going to talk about it, the city is going to say we have this much money to do this with, but most of that money is going to salaries. They're supposed to fix the problem, but really, we're just in this vicious cycle of, 'I'm fixing the problem, I'm fixing the problem,' when really what you're doing is just keeping them homeless. The only solution for homelessness is homes. Get somebody inside, and then get them services."

By this point, Christian had fully dissuaded me of the notion of homelessness as a choice. Yet if you talk to enough kids on the street, you'll find some who will say it was their choice. "I don't like being inside," one kid who went by the name Maggie May told me. Part of it is what Christian has always maintained—that these kids will say it's their choice because nobody wants to admit they're miserable. Part of it is also that life on the streets is still better than a lot of alternatives. And beneath it all lies a desire we all share from time to time, no matter our walk of life: the desire to run away. To be free. To get away from what is bothering you.

"My brain still tells me, 'Fuck, it would be so much easier just to be living in the park again,'" Christian laughed. "And I'm like, 'How is my brain, still after so many years, still directed that way whenever I'm too stressed out with the workload or whatever is going on with my homelife?' It's like, 'It would be so much better to not have to pay bills and just get harassed by police every day!'"

The issue isn't so much about how these kids end up homeless, Christian said, or even whether they're still at the stage where they say they're happy living untethered, living without a set home. It's about making sure they have the option to not be homeless when they grow sick of the hardscrabble life.

"If you're not hurting anyone but yourself, at some point you are hurting yourself to the point that you don't know when it's time to seek help," said Gary McCoy, a former street kid who now does homeless outreach for the city of San Francisco. "There's a point of no return. Everybody gets tired of it at some point. But will you get tired of it before you even realize you're tired of it? Or are you going to be too far gone to realize it needs to be stopped?"

Gary began snorting heroin while he was in high school in Virginia, and his drug use quickly escalated to dealing drugs, shoplifting, and stealing from friends and family in order to fund his habit. He moved to San Francisco when he was twenty-one in hopes of a fresh start—but within a month, he was back to using, this time methamphetamines. He was soon bouncing between friends' couches, flophouses, and the streets. He found a street family who shared his priorities, young kids aged seventeen to twenty-five, and they would run together, trading sexual favors for drugs and finding places to spend the night. "Our life was basically trying to figure out where we would get high next and where we would sleep next," he said. "We'd try and hook up with somebody so we'd have a place to stay for the night. If that didn't work, there were some bushes over there. There was an old overhang, a big awning over a parking lot. A parking garage over by UCSF Parnassus."

He has one specific memory from 2005, when he was twenty-four and had just learned he was HIV positive. He'd gone into the free clinic already high because, in a way, he knew what was coming. And as soon as they confirmed his worst fear, he felt he knew where to go—to his friend's house at the corner of Jones and Geary Streets, and back into the blissful oblivion that is meth, not having to face reality or come to terms with the fact that here he was, homeless and HIV positive and hooked on drugs with seemingly no way out.

"But he wasn't home," Gary said. "I just remember standing there on the corner and spinning. Like, physically spinning, slowly walking in a circle, having no idea what was going to happen. I didn't have anyone to talk to. I couldn't get high because he wasn't home. And I didn't have anywhere to go."

~

All the advocates I spoke with reacted in a similar way when I brought up Haze, Lila, and Sean and the murders they committed in 2015. They'd make a point to separate themselves and other street kids from those three—not every kid is going to end up killing two strangers, and more than anything, this population needs our compassion rather than our fear. They'd wash their hands of the three, and then walk back those statements. ("Nobody is a hopeless case," Christian said.) And then, in walking back that initial visceral response, they can take a step back and put themselves in the trio's shoes and see how any kid could get in over their head in the way that Haze, Lila, and Sean did that week in October 2015. "Once you cross a line, you can cross that line again," Christian said. "My personal opinion, being around death and chaos my entire life—the first killing they did was probably drug-induced weirdness. And once they crossed that line, the next one was, 'Well, that was easy.'"

Beyond anything else, we have to remember that Haze, Lila, and Sean were kids too, prone to the same mob mentality, peer pressure, and groupthink that all kids fall victim to. All kids are guilty of bad ideas, and it is completely dependent on their level of privilege how irreversible and harmful those ideas end up being. Robbery was a line Haze felt comfortable crossing, that all three thought was a reasonable action to take against a young girl they had just met because she was foreign and possibly had money. When they needed a getaway car, they didn't feel bad crossing that line again, this time in Marin County.

All line crossing aside, on the streets, these kids develop a loyalty to each other that runs deep. Too many kids find themselves on the streets because they had no one who showed them enough love to take care of them, so when they find other kids who are willing to fill that familial void, they become attached quickly and without question. By the time they were driving up to Portland in Steve Carter's stolen station wagon, Sean was calling Lila his sister.

For too many, the family they form on the streets is the only family they have, and from that deep bond comes a desperate and unwavering allegiance. There are two sides to that: On one side, there's love, support, comfort, and friendship. There's safety in numbers, there's teamwork, there's strength. But for those who have experienced such little love in their lives, when they finally find it, they will cling to it at all costs. They will lay down their well-being to protect what is theirs. They will disregard the well-being of others for their street family.

Looking back now, Gary can see the danger that comes with finding your street family, when the people for whom you'd do anything are just as unpredictable, volatile, and hurt as you are. "When I was out there, all the guys I was using with, who were giving me free drugs, who I would inject—I was loyal to them," Gary said. "They were my community."

In his homeless outreach, Gary got to know one of the kids involved in a horrific torture and drowning case that took place in Golden Gate Park a few months after the murders of Audrey and Steve. According to prosecutors, at least five transient men and women were involved, the youngest just nineteen and the oldest thirty-seven. "That was a huge shock to me," Gary said. "I felt like he was just following someone else's lead. He was not somebody who would have just gone in and done something unless he thought he needed to because other people told him to."

Gary went on: "But I could see being in that group at Golden Gate Park. I could see being loyal to them. I could see how easy it would be to make one really bad decision and not be able to come back from it, something that might sound like a good idea for a second and you act on it and your entire life is destroyed—and somebody else's if it's a murder."

Far too many street kids lack the luxury to up and leave their little street families, even if they wanted to. Because on the streets, when everything you do is for your survival, your street family is sometimes the only form of protection you have. And there are far worse forces out there looking for ways to hurt you.

NINE

Momo sat apart from the dogs and dirty kids splayed out on the carpet of a living room in Santa Rosa, California, stitching square patches while her five-week-old puppy snoozed on her lap. She and her boyfriend rarely travel to California, she told me, but the Black Sheep Solstice Gathering always takes place somewhere in the state at the end of December. Adam Buxbaum, a thirty-year-old dirty kid active in the Rainbow Family, had opened his home in Santa Rosa for an impromptu potluck as a precursor to the gathering. Momo and the dozens of others who passed through Adam's living room that afternoon all identified as travelers, hippies, drifters, and dirty kids.

Haze had attended a number of annual and regional Rainbow Gatherings through his travels, and befriended many Rainbow regulars while on the road. His mother posted on Haze's Facebook page an update about his sentencing, and Adam commented on that post, offering to publish the address of the jail where Haze was being held in the Rainbow Family newspaper so that other Rainbows could write him. When I reached out to Adam, he explained that he didn't really know Haze. The Rainbow Family functions as more of a leaderless, egalitarian community movement than an organization with a set membership, and in this desultory world where interactions can be both fleeting and lasting at the same time, sometimes it's easier to friend someone on Facebook that you met in passing than to risk never seeing them again. Nonetheless, Adam invited me to the potluck, saying it would be a good opportunity for me to meet "a whole bunch of dirty kids, travelers, and Rainbow hippies at once," and on a Monday afternoon, I found myself driving north to his family home.

I approached the potluck expecting the sort of raucous music and shouted conversation typical of any party, only to find the home as quiet as any other home along the residential street. While the pot, food, and kombucha were plentiful that afternoon, Adam made a point of telling me that the gathering was alcohol- and drug-free—alcohol and hard drugs are a point of contention within the Rainbow community, with some believing they should be banned at the gatherings and others feeling that that would go against the whole free-for-all, anarchist spirit of Rainbow. The only indication that there was anything out of the ordinary taking place in this neighborhood were the two large buses parked alongside Adam's house—one was a former yellow school bus, and the other was painted white, with its name, 42 Skiido, scrawled proudly above the windshield.

Upon my arrival, the dogs greeted me first: big pit bull mixes with names like Petunia and Minnow, a scruffy wirehaired terrier, some tiny yipping Chihuahua types, and a calm thick-furred mutt called Hustle. They rushed the door as I entered, balancing a small cake on top of a large pie—I wasn't really sure what one brings to a potluck of dirty kids. But the get-together wasn't much different from the hangouts I used to have when I was in college, sitting around in my friends' dorm rooms, drinking mixed drinks made with cheap vodka and chatting about nothing. The overall mood was chill and happy, and people greeted each other with deep, lingering hugs. The kids relaxed on the floor, flicking through their phones and passing joints as the weak winter sun gave way to night in a haze of marijuana smoke. Every so often, someone would jump into a side conversation and breathe life into the room, with others interjecting their two cents. Two women piled on a couch entertained the two children who had accompanied their mother, telling them silly jokes that continued long after the children had lost interest: "What did the zero say to the eight? . . . I like your belt."

And then there was Momo. She held herself with a gravitas that made her seem older than the others in the room, but when she drew closer, the pale fragility of her elfin face and her thin limbs hidden under an overly large moss-colored sweater betrayed her youth. "I just turned twenty-one," she chirped in a high, girlish voice. Her hair was growing back shaggy and ash-blonde along the previously shaved side of her head, but the rest was tinged pink. She remained focused on her sewing as the group passed around joints the size of cigars, stopping to take the occasional hit with her head bent over her work.

I asked her about her life, and she opened up in the frank, matter-of-fact way most street kids do when asked to talk about themselves. She ran away from home in Spokane, Washington, at fourteen, to get away from her mother, with whom she was butting heads, and her alcoholic father. "I decided to not be a burden to my dad," she said. "And, well, fuck my mom." Her parents filed a missing person report. She knew that, as an underage missing person, she would put at risk anyone who helped her travel, so she remained in the Spokane area.

"I went to a friend's house that now I realize is a trap house," Momo said. "The upstairs renter person was also in charge of the downstairs, but he was the drug lord person who was doing a bunch of deals. The people who lived downstairs made sure cops wouldn't come inside. But I got to live there. It was free, it was warm, and there was food. I lived there for three months, just for the cold season, and then I went and established two camps by the river in two different places. I ran those camps for the warm seasons for the next two years, and then I was seventeen and a half so I hit the road."

Her birdlike hands flitted over the small blue dolphin she stitched to a cloud-gray patch. "Once I hit the road, I went straight to a gathering and did festivals and stuff, and I came to the realization that the vast majority of the people going to gatherings and festivals and stuff are all really drunk and really high," she said. "I never really wanted to party. I just wanted a nice quiet place to read a book and sew. So I just sew."

With the exception of the two children, Momo was one of the youngest ones there that day. Most of the other Rainbows and dirty kids there had at least half a decade on her, including her thirty-seven-year-old boyfriend, Cory, yet at times, I felt like Momo was the only adult in the room. At one point, ash from an oversize joint spilled onto the carpet, prompting laughs and shouts of "Reefer madness!" "This is why a big joint is not a good idea," Momo said seriously, before giggling. Midway through the afternoon, a dreadlocked kid dressed like a pirate with a long trench coat and feathered hat entered with a burst of energy and a backpack containing eleven twenty-six-day-old puppies. Everyone cooed and squealed as he passed around the tiny black-and-brown fluff balls, so young and shapeless that they still wriggled about like worms. I too got swept up in the excitement, cuddling and petting and playing with the adorable lumps, and the joy soon devolved into a distracted but tempered chaos, with puppies passing through different hands and getting left wherever. Momo watched all this with pursed lips, her own puppy, Decaf, secure in her lap—she knew puppies that young would not have had the proper vaccinations and shouldn't mingle with other dogs or go outdoors. The pirate kid who had brought the puppies in his backpack shrugged off any concerns. "So today is the worst day of their lives," he said. "They're only twenty-six days old." It was Momo who jumped up to stop one wayward pup that was inching closer and closer to the sliding door, all while making sure her own puppy stayed out of the fray.

"She carries herself really well," Cory said, bringing her a thermos of hot tea. "She carries herself better than most adults. She has no desire to do any drugs, LSD or any of them."

"Well, I can't do LSD or mushrooms anymore," she retorted. "I'm retired." She had unknowingly consumed drugs once, she told me, "willfully dosed" by someone with bad intentions. It is why she and Cory run a sober kitchen out of their bus—the white vehicle named 42 Skiido parked out front—to provide a food source that dirty kids can trust. "It's important to know where your food is coming from, and it's better to process it yourself," she said. "People don't have very good intentions. There's types of, for example, trippy LSD kids, that think that dosing a large supply of water is a good idea, and everybody should drink it."

In her case, it had been a burrito. She had just started traveling and was hanging out somewhere in Oregon, with a group not too unlike the one in Adam's living room, when someone handed her a burrito. To this day, that is all she can remember before the drugs hit. "I didn't know" it had drugs in it, she said, "and I was high, really high."

I clucked sympathetically. "Did you not like it?" I asked, feeling like the squarest of squares in a room of topsy-turvy bubble shapes. Adam had passed me a joint earlier, and I demurred, saying I didn't like to smoke while I worked, but the truth is that marijuana makes me sleepy and I don't care for it. I'd had no experience whatsoever with anything stronger than a potent weed brownie while watching *Planet Earth*, and I had no idea what was considered acceptable or unacceptable dosing etiquette. *How do you do, fellow kids?* I chuckled to myself, thinking of the bit where a comically obvious adult Steve Buscemi went undercover as a high schooler.

"I, uh, actually have been fried to a point that if I do hallucinogens, I have seizures," Momo said. "Or I become paralyzed. Mushrooms paralyze me. LSD makes me have seizures."

Could that all happen just from one bad trip? Christ, maybe all that antidrug fearmongering we had to sit through in school has some merit. "All from that burrito?" I asked, stupidly.

Momo paused. "Well, not all from the burrito," she said. "I was scooped up after the burrito and kept high."

"Oh."

You get told a lot of awful things as a journalist, especially when your focus is crime and criminal justice. I've had an inmate at a county jail fall into my arms in tears; I've had mothers describing the messages they receive in dreams from their dead children. You learn quickly in this line of endeavor how to roll with even the most surprising of statements, but in that moment, I honestly didn't know how to react. Momo sat there with such calm, her chubby puppy snoozing blissfully in her lap, telling me how she had been kept high so she could be raped and beaten repeatedly over the course of months. She spoke of this ordeal as casually as if she were disclosing basic facts about herself like her age, or where she was born—as if this weren't the sort of traumatic urban-legend stuff of nightmares that parents tell their children to frighten them into not trusting strangers. I didn't know how to wrap my head around what she was saying to me, and it took me a good few minutes to absorb the full gravity of what she had endured.

I had never heard of something like this happening before I spoke with Momo, but in the months that followed, I heard of nothing else. Every street kid knows of another kid who knew a kid who heard of a situation like this: some homeless kid getting drugged and kidnapped and forced into prostitution. One girl in San Francisco had a friend who had been injected with heroin and kept captive for days before she made a break for it and got out of the house. She also heard rumors of a man going around Buena Vista Park with a needle full of liquid ketamine. "He like shot someone up with ketamine and kidnapped them," she said. Some of the Rainbows I spoke with called it "hippie-napping"—at a regional gathering in Arizona, they stopped a woman from making off with a boy who was too high to consent to leaving. "That's the darker side of what happens when you're out on the street and you don't have the foundation or stability or the protection that a house or a group of people have for you," Momo said.

At the heart of it is a hustle that has existed for as long as mankind has felt entitled to nonconsensual sex, and as is too often the case, those who live on the margins of society are more at risk for sexual exploitation. A man in Ventura County, California, allegedly plied multiple teenage runaway girls with drugs and alcohol over the course of several years so he could sexually assault them. A Michigan man was arrested on suspicion of torturing and abusing a thirteen-year-old runaway with whom he engaged in a sexual relationship for three years. In Massachusetts, three young men and a woman allegedly duct-taped a sixteen-year-old runaway from New Jersey to a chair in their basement, where they drugged her, raped her, beat her, and shaved her head.

Momo estimated that she was held against her will, in a drug-induced state, for anywhere between three and six months. She suspected that her captors had more planned for her—possibly forced prostitution—but she managed to get away before it came to that.

"By the time I escaped, I had completely devolved into animalistic behavior," Momo said. "As a defense mechanism, I shit, pissed, and puked all the time. Nobody wanted to touch me because I would shit, piss, puke, scream, scratch, whatever. It helped and hurt. They would rather beat me into submission or give me something to sedate me. But I wasn't willing. And they knew it."

The potluck continued around us as we spoke, with more and more people coming and going and staying and leaving, unaware of the ugliness we discussed. She told me she had made her way down to San Diego after she escaped, living on Ocean Beach, a hub for drifters and street kids. "The first month of it, I couldn't talk," she said. "I hadn't found out how to talk to people again. Two and a half months into it, a person that had seen me wandering around, picking up trash . . . this guy, River. He picked me up off the street and said, 'I don't know what's wrong with you, but you need some help, and you can come to my house. I'm not going to do anything to you. Come get a shower, sleep. You'll be safe. You'll be fine.' And I did, and I stayed there for about a month, and I came down fully, and I was able to talk again and be somewhat functional in a social situation. Then I decided it was time for me to go on, and I did."

"I worked through a lot of it," she said. "I'm still working through it every day. But yeah, it fucked me up."

I asked her whether she felt any residual bitterness or anger over what she had gone through, and true to form, she looked upon her experience pragmatically. She said she felt disappointed that this had happened to her—"disappointed," as if her captors had forgotten to do their chores rather than drugging and raping her. "We live in a world where, when somebody beats you down and brutally rapes you and treats you like a dog for months, it's unheard of," she said. "But on the opposite side of that, if you look at humans historically, we have always been this way. We have always raped and murdered each other. We have always stolen, always warred. That's how it is."

It was almost like the conversation I had with Haze, in which I sought any kind of reaction or emotion from him over the murder of Audrey Carey. I found myself pushing Momo, seeking more than pragmatism, more than logic. Instead, I was met with just more calm. "Not everyone is mentally capable of going through trauma without breaking," she said. "I'm really happy that everything fucked-up in my life happened to me. I know a lot of other women would be a lot more broken. A lot of other women would not be able to handle it."

Perhaps I would have been one of those women. For weeks after learning of Momo's ordeal, I couldn't stop thinking of what had happened to her. On the nights when my eyes refused to close, I found myself fixated on justice, on finding these villains and holding them accountable for hurting young girls. *Could this be some kind of underworld street kid sex trafficking ring?* I wondered. Momo had no idea who her captors were—whether they were fellow street kids or just predators who preyed on street kids—or even where in Oregon this had all taken place. When I was in Portland, Oregon, I asked Miriam Montes, a former street kid who now runs the St. Francis of Assisi Dining Hall, what she knew of a possible local street kid trafficking ring. She shrugged. "A lot of women come in here and share with me that they were dosed, or someone would be like, 'Hey, let's go get high,' and then they get them high and have their way with them regardless of what they say.

"The women out here are victimized constantly," Miriam said. "They're raped, they're beaten. I can think of one or two off the top of my head who would rather pee on themselves and smell like stale urine as a defense mechanism, rather than be clean and get raped."

When I headed into the downtown area near the river, where most of the city's homeless encampments pop up, I got similar heartbreaking answers.

"Oh yeah!" said a thirty-one-year-old homeless woman who asked to be identified only as Stephanie. "My friend just got raped on the other side of the bridge the other night."

I asked her whether her friend had been raped by other street kids. "Yeah," she said. "It's pretty much people stealing from their own people, people hurting their own people."

The unfortunate truth is that this sort of exploitation probably happens more often than we know. It's just that the kids that it happens to are most likely kids who are already missing—kids who aren't going to report a crime. Kids whose disappearance we're not going to notice. Kids hurting each other and hurting themselves. Hurt people hurt people, or so the old adage goes, and far too many of the transient youth we pass on the streets each day have been hurt, at some point or another. I left my conversation with Momo thinking that what had happened to her had been an atrocious anomaly, only to learn that it was all too common within this community.

A UC Berkeley study tracking homeless youth in San Francisco over the course of six years found that street kids experience a mortality rate in excess of ten times that of the state's general youth population, but the public rarely hears about these statistics. The fact that there haven't been more stories about these victimized kids doesn't mean this cycle of hurt isn't still turning. It means that we only pay attention when the cycle's radius spins wild and wide enough to affect us, the ones with homes and jobs and stability—when the person hurt or killed is someone outside the homeless or street kid community. After Audrey Carey's body was found in Golden Gate Park, local news was slow to report out the details, not just because it had happened over one of the busiest weekends in the city, but because many—including myself, I regret to admit—wrote her death off as yet another homeless-on-homeless crime gone awry. Such stories flow out of Golden Gate Park and other areas frequented by this population daily—drug overdoses, fights, stabbings, and worse.

Six months after Audrey's murder, a city gardener discovered the body of Stephen Williams, a sixty-six-year-old homeless man, floating in Alvord Lake, a small body of water at the entrance of the park near Stanyan Street known fondly among the street kids as "Hep C Pond." This was the torture and drowning case Gary had spoken of, involving a kid he had tried to help get off the streets. Authorities said these five transient men and women tortured, beat, and drowned Williams over the course of three days before he succumbed to "multiple traumatic injuries" and his assailants tossed his body in the pond. A sixth man was charged with assault and conspiracy in connection with the slaying. The group killed Williams as a form of "street justice," investigators said—they believed he had masturbated near children in the park, an unforgivable act in the realm of street kids. But despite the complexities and multiple people behind this killing, Williams's death didn't get nearly the media attention that the killings of Audrey Carey and Steve Carter received. It wasn't until police announced the arrests of two additional suspects more than two months after the initial arrests of nineteen-year-old Stephen Billingsley, alias "Pizza Steve," and thirty-seven-year-old Nikki Lee Williams, who goes by the nickname "Evil," that many of us in the local media even realized that police had arrested another street kid on suspicion of murder and the other person on suspicion of assault and conspiracy.

Like so many transient kids before him, Haze Lampley experienced his share of hurts on the streets, and especially, on the road. And, just like so many other transient kids before, Haze did his share of hurting as well. One night in Snowville, Utah, a drunk kid who "hella looked like Kevin Bacon" started tussling with him over a girl. "So I smashed his face with a beer bottle," he said. He mentioned in passing that after that, he got taken in by an older woman in Ogden, Utah—"Old people like young street kids," he said—but was reluctant to get into the details of this story or the specifics of the arrangement. Eventually he revealed that he'd had to sneak away from her home in the dead of night, wearing nothing but a pair of long shorts and a T-shirt, despite it being the middle of winter.

Once, while traveling through New Mexico, he'd teamed up with a female drifter who had almost gotten raped during her last ride. He'd agreed to help keep her safe, and within hours into their first ride, he'd had to pull out the gun. "We got picked up, and the guy just starts coming onto the girl, putting his hand on her leg," he said. "I pulled out the gun and said, 'Hey buddy, look in your mirror,' and he was all, 'Hey, hey, you don't have to do that.' I told him to pull over. He pulled over in the middle of the highway, but he just sat there and wouldn't leave. So I shot out his taillight and he drove off with the doors still open."

Not long after that, a man who had picked Haze up while he was hitchhiking in Colorado tried to rape him. "He looked like a regular dude," Haze said. "He smoked pot, offered me a couple of brews. My beer was in the cupholder because I had my pack on my lap. I only drank one beer and then I was out. I woke up feeling him pulling my pants down.

"I just swung," Haze said. "I broke two of his teeth. I took his wallet, his keys, his car, and his cell phone. I almost took his shoes."

Haze told the story of his near rape in the same matter-of-fact manner as that of the girl he had protected in New Mexico—it was as if it hadn't happened to him, but to someone else. He talked about what he did in both instances with enthusiasm, laughing about how he'd taken care of those who'd dared to cross him. He said he drove the car of the man who tried to rape him back to San Diego, where he dumped it in the ocean—a dubious claim for him to make, given how beloved and protected California's beaches are, not to mention the fact that he maintains he is deathly afraid of being behind a wheel—and then used the man's debit card to take out thousands of dollars in cash. When I expressed skepticism, questioning how he was able to withdraw cash without the man's PIN, and indeed well beyond the typical ATM withdrawal limit, he doubled down, saying that some debit cards didn't need PINs.

It was such an odd detail not just to lie about, but to stand behind when he was called out on it. These were the sorts of moments that gave me pause when it came to weighing the truthfulness in Haze's telling of his life story. It reminded me of one of the few times I babysat as a teenager, when a little girl I was supposed to be watching kicked a little boy in the face (I was a terrible babysitter). "Are you OK?" I asked the boy, as he stood in shock. "Yeah," he said, tentatively touching his mouth. "Are you hurt?" I asked. "No," he scoffed, blood bubbling from his lip. I got the impression that Haze was trying to outman his attempted rapist—that his bravado and lies were just him trying to prove that even though this man had hurt him, he'd hurt the man more.

Because if there was one thing Haze had learned early on in his life, it was that if you're not the one doing the hurting, then you're the one getting hurt.

TEN

Under the Rainbow

Regardless of the different families and groups that gather in every hub, street kid communities tend to take on different personalities from city to city. San Francisco has the Haight Kids, the hippies, and the Deadheads, while San Diego has a more skateboarder and surfer vibe. The street kids in New Orleans are known as "gutter punks," "crusties," or "scum fucks" and have a more punk, anarchist feel than street kids from elsewhere.

But street kids and travelers from all walks of life seem to always find their way to the Rainbow Family of Living Light, a leaderless, egalitarian community that comes together at counterculture-steeped gatherings on public lands throughout the country and the world, typically in nature. The annual Rainbow Gathering can draw up to thirty thousand people and takes place at a predetermined, consensus-approved location each July. Smaller regional gatherings can happen at various points throughout the year.

It's with Rainbow that a lot of the misconceptions around home-less youth originate. All are welcome at Rainbow Gatherings, including "housies," people who live indoors, but the overall philosophy behind this free-living society that was founded in 1970 attracts a lot of aging hippies, New Age earth mothers, freegans, peaceniks, and the "trustafarian" archetypes that street kids get lumped in with—hippies who believe in living free but also have resources and a brick-and-mortar home base. While some Rainbows may play at being homeless and have support systems to fall back on when they get tired of wandering, dirty kids and former street kids make up the overwhelming majority, said Michael Niman, the Buffalo State College journalism professor who authored *People of the Rainbow: A Nomadic Utopia*.

"These are kids who are running away from some really, really ugly, grisly shit," Niman said. "There is no home to go back to. Home was violence. Home was sexual abuse. Rainbow gave them a safe haven."

Rainbow Gatherings take the concept of a street family to the nth degree, providing kids with a whole functioning infrastructure for weeks at a time, in which they can fully be themselves. A Rainbow Gathering is a guaranteed week or two of access to necessities that these kids usually have to fight for—food, shelter, medical care. But more than anything, Niman said, with the Rainbows, street kids get to exist as themselves, unapologetically. They won't get hassled for sitting in a public place while looking grungy, or be kicked out of yoga for having body odor. They won't get sneered at for asking for food or water, or treated like a charity case when they seek help.

"It's the only place they can go where they will be accepted by somebody other than a social worker," Niman said. "Their whole identity is criminalized, but at Rainbow, you're a human for two weeks, and then you go back to being a piece of shit that nobody will look at." Rainbows greet newcomers at the gatherings with, "Welcome home!" Attending a gathering is referred to as "heading home" or "going home." It's clear why such a meetup would draw in so many homeless kids, many of whom have no concept of what a home is, or what it means to be welcomed into one.

Adam Buxbaum, the Rainbow who hosted a potluck in his home in Santa Rosa, extended an invitation to me to attend the regional

Valentine's Day Gathering in Arizona. Though Adam considers himself a dirty kid, and though he travels extensively, wandering from gatherings to festivals to Grateful Dead shows with his wirehaired terrier mix, Mr. Magpie, in tow, he's not someone I would categorize as homeless. He has his family-owned home and enough wherewithal to earn the money he needs to travel, albeit cheaply. His wandering has even taken him outside the country, to world Rainbow Gatherings in Taiwan and to visit friends he met on the road in Europe. "I'm one of the more privileged travelers," he acknowledged. "I know how to live like a bum but in an emergency, I don't have to. I can go home."

But Adam gave the impression of being one of the true believers in the Rainbow lifestyle and philosophy, and he is always eager to share that with others. He told me the regional gathering would be a good way for me to get my toes wet and meet a bunch of street kids all at once.

Every decision within the Rainbow Family requires unanimous consensus, making for a sometimes lengthy and complicated process. For the annual and regional gatherings, there's always a general date and then a consensus council meeting to decide the location. Volunteers will scout out campsites at predetermined, consensus-approved locations a few weeks before each gathering, and through word of mouth, Rainbows figure out where to go and how to get there.

As a rule, Rainbows never publish the location or coordinates of their camp, and they go to great lengths to inform only those who plan on going. They don't believe in getting permits and allowing the federal government to dictate the terms of their gatherings, and the secrecy prevents any interference from local law enforcement. In the Facebook group for the Arizona Gathering, administrators took down several posts that shared the coordinates of the camp ahead of the gathering in Tonto National Forest.

Regional gatherings tend to be smaller than the annual festivities, and this one drew only a few hundred. But the setup, deep in the belly of Tonto National Forest, was impressive. The camp was located miles off the main roads, accessible only by a winding dirt road whose bumps and divots thumped and shook every motorist making the drive in. Giant cacti lined the path to the camp, their crooked arms outstretched as if in greeting; javelina scurried through the kicked-up clouds of dirt. Someone had set up a cheery but windbeaten "Welcome" sign at the entrance to camp, but several massive SUVs from the local sheriff's office had blocked it from view upon my arrival.

As with any gathering, the A Camp—the camp for alcoholics—was located closest to the entrance, to serve as a buffer for the rest of the camp against the outside world. A Camp looked like a tailgate, with people sitting by their cars and drinking, and so did the limbo lot next to it that wasn't part of A Camp but wasn't entirely part of the main camp either.

I approached the camp with trepidation, having never done anything quite like this before. My nerves were frayed from navigating the bumpy road in a stupidly bright-blue Hyundai rental that was not equipped for this level of off-roading, and the extra parking lot confused me. But the slim grizzled gentleman from "big bad A Camp" pointed me in the direction of parking, and I eased the rental car past prickly bushes and around dogs lounging wherever they had felt like plopping down. I stopped in front of one woman relaxing in a foldout chair by her car with her large black-and-tan mutt, whose paws were poking out into the narrow pathway left clear for cars. I rolled down my window. "Do I have enough room?" I asked. "You're good," she said. I inched forward, and the dog let out a yelp. "Holy shit, did I get her? Oh god! I'm so sorry. Is she OK?" The woman patted the dog, who had yanked her paws back and resettled next to her. "She's fine. I think you got like the tip of her toe or something." I felt awful but didn't know what else to do, so I kept going until I reached the back of the lot. When I got out of the car, I realized that power lines ran above the lot; a constant clicking buzz of energy was vibrating through the air over our heads.

Dusty, a bulky woman with short bright hair and a samurai sword the length of her lower body holstered at her hip, volunteered to take me to the main camp. She pulled with her a small cart full of old clothes, hollering, "Warm clothes for cold people!" to everyone she passed. Her droopy basset hound, Lou, came with us. Dusty's sword dragged on the ground behind her as we walked; Lou's long ears and sagging teats did the same.

Niman warned me that when I got to camp, I would "feel light in a way that's difficult to describe." "You'll feel high without smoking anything," he had said. "You'll feel safe if everything is working properly. Everybody will say hello to you." People greeted us with a "welcome home" here and there, as we slowly shuffled farther down the road, where the bright and colorful buses were parked and the campfires had begun to pop up around the site. "It's gorgeous," Dusty said when we reached the lot. Children ran around and played by themselves, supervised by one or two adults at a time. They crowded Dusty's cart, a ready-made dress-up factory, pulling out this and that and holding items of clothing up to themselves. "That's so you," a woman giggled as a little girl contemplated a red-and-white fuzzy Santa jacket.

A makeshift bridge served as a dry crossing over the creek, which would be the camp's main water source that week, and as the entry point into the main portion of the gathering. Stacked rocks marked the trail up into the camp, past a clean water station and through a thicket of trees. Dusty took me to the main circle, where everyone gathered twice a day for meals. The circle wasn't in use when we got there, and a few kids were taking advantage of the open space to lounge around. I had expected more people and activity at the base camp, but people mostly clumped into little groups. Niman's book had prepared me for kitchens and medical centers, but I hadn't been able to spot either of those. I had lugged with me a twenty-pound bag of rice and a large cylinder of oatmeal to contribute to the group, and I left that in the circle so I could set up my tent before dark.

Adam was right in that there was no shortage of street kids. I could plop down at any campfire and get twenty different stories about homelessness and living that drifter lifestyle. Many of the kids I spoke with described the same tough upbringings of abuse and neglect that the kids I spoke with in San Francisco and San Diego had experienced. Around a campfire one night, over a discussion about washing a kid's mouth out with soap, somebody made a crack about how his parents had never abused him, and the rest of the circle responded by ragging on him: "Ohhh, look at this guy with parents who weren't abusive!"

"Rainbow is a really healing thing for the travely kids," said Nathan Akre, twenty-nine, who came across Rainbow in his younger years, when he was constantly running away from his "toxic" family in Idaho. "It's the poets of the night, the people who have nowhere to go. They are able to take solace in each other's company because they have nothing."

The flip side to that, however, were the kids' worried families. In the Facebook group for the gathering, a variety of similar posts emerged among the messages of love and belonging.

> Has anyone at the gathering talked to or seen a guy named Jeremiah?

> If anyone has seen Terrence, please let me know and also ask him to call his family.

> Her name is Alene . . . her family won't stop calling me.

> Please be on the look out for this man. He is believed to be in danger of harming himself, and his family is worried about him.

For as long as these avenues have existed, these sorts of pleas have popped up on all kinds of online message boards and social media groups for transient living. In a time when it's easier than ever to know where somebody is at all times of the day, it also appears to be easier than ever to disappear.

One woman was particularly persistent in her posts, asking anyone for any information about her "baby daughter." She put up photo after photo of a dusky, sullen young girl of Asian descent who seemed incapable of smiling. Even with silly Snapchat filters of flower crowns, she looked pained, her lips stretched tight and her dark eyes blank.

"Becky, it's Chinese New Year," the mother wrote. "Come back, please."

Some responded to her pleas, asking whether her daughter also went by the name Echo. The mother had no idea, but at the evening circle one night, there she was, small and unsmiling in an oversize sweatshirt. There was a core group of women she seemed to have attached herself to, and she was laying her head on their shoulders and cuddling up with them in the sweet way that all Rainbows show affection.

Later that night, as I sat by the campfire at I Dunno Café, a kitchen that serves strong fair-trade coffee at gatherings, Adam noticed Echo walking by and called out to her. It was just after the sun had set, and a sense of calm had fallen across the main camp. The evening meal at the main circle had finished up, and people were peeling off to sit around their chosen campfires. Musicians had pulled out their instruments and filled the air with light strumming and jaunty little ukulele ditties. The dogs, fed and sated, snuggled up to the humans, who were passing around joints and hand-rolled American Spirits. In the distance, the rowdiness of the more party-minded camps across the creek had started to pick up, with raucous hoots and howls piercing through the cooling air.

"Hey, Echo," Adam said. "Your mom is looking for you."

Echo paused for just a moment. "Yeah, well, my mom's a bitch!" she laughed. She didn't wait for a response before walking away toward the party camps.

The few that had gathered around the campfire grew quiet. "That's not funny," someone muttered. Like so many Rainbows, many that sat around the campfire that night had mothers who actually were bitches. Many there would have loved to have had a mother who worried about their whereabouts, who searched for them when they were lost. Many there would have loved to have had a mother who cared.

By the next morning, Echo wasn't laughing anymore. The sky was still pink, and the majority of the camp still in their sleeping bags as she cut through the main meadow, tearful and shivering, and mumbling to herself. "Are you OK?" I asked, passing her on my way to get some coffee. She snapped out of her agitation for a beat to flash a tight smile, her face still wet with tears. "I'm fine!" she said, her eyes looking past me. She continued her path through the circle, mumbling to herself once again.

Nobody was at I Dunno Café when I got there, so I went over to the next campfire, where Snowflake, a twenty-five-year-old recovering meth addict from Denver, sat half-asleep. Someone had just stoked the flames awake, the damp wood spewing more ash and smoke than fire. A few others had joined our circle when a kid walked by with Echo, who was still crying and talking to herself. "Is she OK?" someone asked, as she abruptly plopped into an empty canvas chair by the fire. "She's all right," the other kid replied. "We're going to the main meadow to do some balancing."

"It's flooding me," Echo rambled. "All the things, all at once, and I can't help it. I just can't. I just can't. I can't. I can't help it. Happy Valentine's Day. It's your birthday. Happy Valentine's Day. Every day is Valentine's Day. If you come to Arizona, bring water. Bring water, bring wood. I just want, I just want everybody to be on their game. We have so much shit to do."

Echo wrapped her arms around her legs and rested her face on her knees. "Are you OK? Do you need a hug?" another kid asked.

"Someone is passing around some bad drugs," someone cracked, but somebody else remarked that she hadn't slept in four days.

"Damn. She needs to sleep."

"It's not like that though. She just has a higher vibration."

"People assume."

She kept up her mumbling and crying as everybody tried to carry on side conversations and continue business as usual. Some jumped into her ramblings, engaging her and attempting to follow her train of thought.

"I keep saying put some fire on the fire because it's firewood and it's already fire," she said. "Wood is so fire it's fire already. You can make so many things from the wood of the earth. You know what's another word for love? *Bliss*. You know what's another word for bliss? *Spoons*. You know what's another word for spoons? *Eyes*. We're all just love. We're all just one, right?"

"I like her analogies and her connections and how she sees things," Snowflake drawled. "It's cool."

"This is like small circles, right?" Echo said. "It's like putting all the elements. It's like little campfires everywhere. You got campfires in the sky, you got campfires down here."

"Everything comes back full circle," a man responded.

"That's why it's called circles," she said. "My name would be Circles whenever it needs to be. Circles."

"So would you like to be called Arrow, or Circles, or Echo?"

"They're all our names," she said. "But I think, right now, I should be Arrow."

Maybe it was bad drugs, but almost everybody at the Rainbow Gathering has been around others in such a state long enough to recognize it for something more: "Schizophrenia," someone whispered as Echo quietly sang Bob Marley to herself.

"Don't you worry, about a thing," she whispered, her face still pressed into her knees. "'Cause every little thing is going to be all right. Don't you worry. About a thing. 'Cause every little thing is going to be OK."

Later, a less tearful but still babbling Echo-Maybe Arrow-Maybe Circles made her way back to I Dunno Café, where I sat sipping coffee. "I am the void into which God speaks," she told the people at that fire. "That's why I'm Echo." As at the first campfire, the few there kept with business as usual while also making sure she had water and food. The Rainbows seemed to have enough experience with people in a state of psychosis, caused perhaps by mental illness or brought on by drugs, and knew to let it just ride out. But in a moment of comfortable silence, Echo asked, with a ringing clarity, "When is my mom going to get here?"

"When is my mom going to get here?" For days after I'd left the gathering, those eight words refused to stop rolling around in my head. I couldn't say with certainty how old Echo was—after a while, these kids all take on the same weathered yet ageless look—but the sentiment behind those eight words was so simple, so pure. It's the first thought we have upon entering this world: "I want my mommy."

If only it were that simple. But nothing in the world of street kids is ever simple. In this world, there is no good and there is no evil, no clear-cut villain or straightforward hero. The good guys have all done bad things, and the bad guys have layers to them; nothing is purely black and nothing purely white.

Those few days I was at the Rainbow Gathering, my own mother had hounded me for updates that I was safe, that I hadn't fallen victim to a murderous hippie cult in the middle of the desert. "You know I'm almost thirty, right?" I'd hissed over the phone before the gathering. "Yes, but you'll always be my baby," she replied. The concern that Echo's mother had for her daughter was not unfamiliar to me, and I considered, for the first time in my career, stepping away from my role as an objective observer and reaching out to her mother to make sure Echo got the help she needed.

Because Echo needed help. That was clear. She was possibly suffering from a mental illness, and she was possibly taking psychedelics that were only exacerbating her psychosis. But Echo's mother was not my mother, who I know with the certainty of the DNA she gave me loves me beyond her own being. If I had been Echo, I would have wanted someone to contact my mother, who would have trekked through the wilds of Arizona to rescue me, her almost-thirty-year-old baby, from the evil, evil hippies.

Echo's mother could not be the one to give her the help that she needed. After her initial pleas, her mother began to show her colors, inundating the Facebook group with odd, manipulative statements. She implied that Echo was selfish for not calling about her grandfather's health or being with her family for Chinese New Year, and she hinted that she was filing a missing person report.

"Mom was obviously overbearing," Adam said. He had responded to some of the mother's posts and spoken to Echo about her mother's concerns. "If there are minors who show up at gatherings, we will do anything we can to get them back to their parents. But she's an adult. Echo was clearly going through stuff, but she was also competent. She was figuring out stuff, she was making plans to leave. If somebody wasn't competent, we take it more seriously."

~

What I learned at this gathering was that, for a lot of the kids, traveling and living on the streets was how they figured it out. It felt preposterous, this notion that being homeless would help in the long run. But for some of these kids, it's what they needed to do. It was the better option in a life with shit options. Sometimes it's better to figure it out on the road than to figure it out within four walls where you have a warm bed and steady meals but none of the security and safety that is supposed to come with a home.

"If you're running away from something long enough, you will eventually run to something else," said Sleepy, the thirty-seven-year-old proprietor of I Dunno Café who started traveling at fifteen to escape both juvenile hall and a rough homelife. "With more experiences and meeting more people, you're going to find more connections, and that increases your odds of finding something better. I know a lot of these kids out here, they come from really rough backgrounds. A lot of the road family had a rough time growing up. Sometimes, walking it off is what you got to do."

But as it is on the streets, putting together a bunch of traumatized kids working through their own baggage can have dangerous consequences. So many of the kids I spoke with at that gathering had bruises and half-healed scrapes and cuts that they could only have sustained from another human. One kid had two black eyes, and when I made a comment about it, his girlfriend joked, "Well, he deserved it." I witnessed several dogs getting into snarling fights with other dogs, prompting their owners to jump into the fray, which meant taking bites and scratches in order to separate them.

A man posted in the Facebook group that his girlfriend had been sexually assaulted at the gathering by a man named Tonto, who then tossed her out of his tent without her pants or underwear. While one man expressed regret that nobody did anything to stop the assault, somebody else posted that the girl had been high and "shoulda kept the needle out of her arm." He continued: "I'm not helping to serve justice for tweakers." Whatever the outcome or actual facts of what happened to that girl, sexual assault was enough of a concern that some Rainbows led a "consent is sexy" campaign that included talks at the evening circle and painting "no means no" on rocks.

The nights could get raucous and rowdy. From the main site, I could hear the sounds of loud music, shouting, laughing, and other party shenanigans emanating from the other side of the creek, closer to where A Camp sat. Drug use is a touchy subject in the Rainbow community—while weed and cigarettes are acceptable, there's never been a consensus on other substances. Snowflake admitted that he crawled into someone's tent at Rainbow that smelled so strongly like the meth he craved that he felt tempted once again. A kid was almost "hippie-napped" at this gathering—he was high, and people he didn't know tried to get him to leave with them—but his friends were able to keep him from being taken.

I thought all the alcohol would stay in A Camp, but I saw kids wandering through the main camp with cans of beer in their hands. The limbo lot next to A Camp imbibed particularly heavily, to the point that so many empty beer cans were piled next to one van that swarms of bees arrived. At the same time, when I sat down for a tarot-card reading at trade circle—a hub for Rainbows to trade and barter, mostly crystals and gems and things of that sort—I offered the kid doing my reading a can of beer in exchange for his services, and he responded with shock. "I don't drink," he said. I gave him a cool-looking rock instead—black with white dots—and he got excited over it as if I hadn't just found it by my tent that morning. He drew the moon, the king of staffs, justice, and the world. "You just had a recent awakening of self," he said. "In the past, you were searching for justice. You will get your justice."

I had planned to meet up with Momo at this gathering, the girl in Santa Rosa who had been drugged, kidnapped, and raped. I was leaving for Portland soon after the gathering, and I wanted to find out more about her ordeal. I wanted to find my justice. But she'd gone into septic shock that required emergency surgery—she'd told me she had been having problems with her kidneys—and her mother had flown her back to Washington so she could get treatment and rest.

I remember thinking back in Santa Rosa that, after what she had gone through, she needed to go someplace stable that could be her home, someplace where she could regroup and recover. She told me she'd returned home to Spokane a few times to try "normal life," and no matter what, it never worked out. "I was just so unhappy," she said. "Everyday society life of a box and a bullshit job that you don't like that gives you paper currency that doesn't fulfill you . . . it doesn't have to be the way that people think it's supposed to be. Because it's not supposed to be this way. The world is falling apart because we think it has to be this way, and it's not healthy."

For her, that stable place wasn't in Spokane, with a job and an apartment and her family. For her, it was on her bus with Cory, on the road, seeing new things, meeting new people, and having new experiences. "The bus goes where I want it to," she said proudly. "I decided that I wanted to travel all the time. Ever since I decided that, I always pictured myself with a male driver on a bus that was ours. I never had the idea that we were in like a completely tied-down committed, 'this is my husband' relationship, but it was more like, 'This is my driver. This is my copilot. This is my bus. This is what we do.' That's exactly what it is. I'm living out what I dreamed."

Rainbow wasn't perfect—nothing is—but I left the gathering feeling more optimistic than I usually do after talking with street kids. I felt gratified that for these kids with so few options, there was something like this—something where they could be who they were, unapologetically, and meet other people who understand and have experienced the same pain that they have.

Dave had been on his way here, I remembered on my way back to California. Way back in 2011, when he'd first opened my eyes to the world of street kids, Dave told me he was on his way to the annual Rainbow Gathering in Washington State. I had no idea what Rainbow was at that time, but in my scant notes, I had jotted down "traveler kids" and "just a bunch of people getting together in the woods and not getting fucked with."

As I drove my stupidly bright-blue rental car, now stupidly scratched up and covered in desert dust, I felt heartened thinking about what Dave would have found if he'd made it to that gathering in 2011. Maybe he'd met Sleepy, who, like so many who were homeless in their youth, ended up working with runaway kids for some time outside of Rainbow, counseling them and connecting them with the services they needed. Maybe he'd met that kind kid who'd been trying to help Echo, or the other one who'd made sure she had water, or that other kid who'd made a point to make sure she knew she was loved as she struggled through that tangled and terrifying state of mind.

Or maybe he'd met Haze.

~

Haze described his time on the road as the closest thing to "running away and joining the circus" that you can get in this day and age. He'd earned enough money for drugs and alcohol through panhandling and doing seasonal work as a picker and stemmer on pot farms, where he'd met many of the Rainbows he'd run with during his travels. He'd attended several regional gatherings and rolled around from "gypsy camp" to gypsy camp, going to music festivals and Grateful Dead shows and "giant parties." "Just love, happiness, and drugs," he said.

Travel is surprisingly easy for those with limited resources but limitless time. Though hitchhiking has dropped off markedly since its heyday in the 1970s, vagabonds and wanderers can still get around by just sticking out their thumbs. Train hopping remains popular as well, especially among the more adventurous, even in a post-9/11 world of increased security. Some are able to team up and save enough money to repurpose old school buses and RVs, and to travel together like that.

And with the advent of social media, it's become easier than ever for travelers to find like-minded communities wherever they go, and to get advice on how best to get to where they want to go. As I traveled around to more street kid hubs and met with drifters, I'd connect with them on Facebook afterward and marvel at how many random friends we'd have in common—other kids I'd met in other locations, thousands of miles away.

Each kid has a different reason for wanting to explore. Some called it "itchy feet," some attributed it simply to the thrill of being young and having the whole world in front of you. Some said they were looking for something, while others seemed to be looking to just get away. For a number of kids I spoke with, it's also just something to do. "Sometimes it's easier to travel than it is to be on the street because if you're traveling, people will take you in and you can stay places," Mindi said. "Otherwise you're just homeless somewhere."

For Haze, the vagabond life was something he inherited from his mother and grandfather. "Wanderlust was something imposed onto me, and then it became natural," he said. "It kept me entertained, and I have to entertain myself, all day, every day, so the anxiety doesn't catch up to me."

Haze claims to have traveled to all fifty states, making it to Alaska "on a trash barge with some water and weed." Like so many of his claims, this one seemed dubious—he said he never had any form of identification, and therefore would never have been able to get on an airplane, yet he'd somehow also made it to Hawaii. Sean Angold was more realistic in his estimations, limiting his travels to only the forty-eight mainland states and Mexico.

Sure, there will always be bad moments on the road. One kid I met at the gathering once accidentally left his banjo behind in Asheville, North Carolina, and had to return to get it in the rain, in a trip that added several days to his journey. For Haze, there was the attempted rape, the violence, and getting stranded in secluded areas. But everything always seems to work out in the end, when you're doing what you feel you're supposed to be doing with your life. Everything always seems to work out when you can run away from what is hurting you rather than confront it head-on.

When Haze ran off in the middle of winter in Ogden, Utah, to get away from the older woman who had taken him in, he got to the nearest rest stop and waited for his next ride out. He sat shivering in nothing but a pair of long shorts and a T-shirt. He tried to bum a cigarette from a passing trucker, who took pity on him and threw him a whole pack of cigarettes and a pair of sweatpants instead.

"Where are you going?" the trucker asked.

"Anywhere but here," Haze replied.

ELEVEN

Corcoran, California
Spring 2018

Corcoran bills itself as both "a great place to raise a family" and "the Farming Capital of California," but it's the latter that the city with a population of twenty-five thousand displays on a large stone sign in the midst of the green fields and tree orchards that stretch out for miles and miles under an endless sky. Located smack-dab in the middle of the state, far from the forest-lush mountains that tower in the distance and the salt-tinged air of the ocean, few paved roads run through these lands. As you drive through this stitchwork grid of farms and fields, passing horses, cows, and goats corralled on the sides of homes and barns, the cities and towns fade into one another in a blur of tranquility and manure-tinged air.

This is the last place anyone would expect to find a street kid like Haze Lampley, but while agriculture makes up much of this county's labor force, a significant portion of the economy is fueled by the two state prisons built among this idyllic heartland. There's Corcoran State Prison, a male-only facility with a history of inmate brutality and poor living conditions that once housed the late cult leader and convicted serial killer Charles Manson, as well as Phillip Garrido, the man behind the Jaycee Dugard abduction. Sean Angold was housed at this prison for his first few years.

Next door is the newer California Substance Abuse Treatment Facility, where Haze is expected to live out his sentence. *Iron Man* actor Robert Downey Jr. served a year of his drug-related conviction here.

On a clear spring Saturday, the visitation room at the treatment facility was bustling with inmates and their families. With so many men in the prison-issued blue pants and shirt, the room seemed tinged in the shade, even as the relentless sun blasted in through the side windows.

The room smelled like a grade-school cafeteria, with the microwaves whirring and beeping with vending machine goodies purchased by visiting loved ones. In the far corner was a mural of a flower-laden archway that opened to an ethereal scene of a body of water at sunset. The mural was for families to pose in front of for photos, but it felt almost like a mockery in this place of little beauty, where rotating fans blew nonstop to dissipate the stale air and body heat of dozens of people packed into a small space. But visiting day means laughter and happiness, children playing with their fathers, and lovers secretly holding hands out of sight of the guards. The goodwill was contagious, even for Haze.

Haze entered the room with the air of someone unsure of what was waiting for him, but he appeared fuller and less withdrawn than he had during the trial. His behavior reflected that change. He laughed freely and rambled on about nothing, whereas before, conversation had had to be dragged from him with extensive coaxing. With his hair cut short, save for one single long dreadlock, there was a reddish sheen to it. His square black frames were of better quality than the pair he had squinted through during the trial.

I'd met with him once, two years earlier, in Marin County Jail. He'd had trouble making eye contact then and spoke slowly, almost in a dazed manner. He'd blamed that on the solitary confinement, under which he was held for most of his stay because the jailhouse deputies had deemed him too dangerous to mingle with the general population.

"Yeah, they thought I was going to start a riot," he scoffed in the Corcoran visiting room, playing with a SoBe iced tea I'd gotten for him from the vending machine. "What are you looking at?" the cap on his tea read.

"Would you have?" I asked.

He shrugged. "Maybe if they hadn't taken the death penalty off the table."

When I spoke with him in Marin County, the trial was still ongoing, and under advice from his attorneys, Haze declined to talk about the killings. We met just once, when he gave me the most cursory glance into his upbringing and his aimless existence as one of the country's millions of homeless youth, sleeping wherever he wouldn't be bothered, shooting up and smoking whatever he could get to pass the time, and scrapping, fighting, stealing, and worse just to survive. That hour-long conversation, combined with the dozens of interviews I'd had with street kids, former street kids, youth psychologists, and homeless advocates had prepared me to expect the worst of the worst when we did meet again. I knew that these would not be easy conversations, and I readied myself the best I could, but in the end, it felt about the same as watching a documentary on hurricanes and then venturing out into the eye of the storm with just an umbrella.

~

One lesson Haze's mother imparted to him that he has closely adhered to all his life was "no snitching," whether it was to the cops, to medical professionals, or to any other kind of authority figure in his life—even those who wanted to help him. Because with the power to help comes the power to hurt, and he has spent the majority of his life bearing the brunt of the latter.

All this raised concerns for me on how truthful his account would be. Haze told me early on that he had "never been honest with a therapist." When I asked him how I would know whether he was lying to me, he asked, "What reason do I have to?"

Well, he has several reasons, actually. Not long after he was sentenced to one hundred years to life in prison, a sentence that meant he would most likely die before he would get a chance to argue his case before a parole board, California changed its youthful offender program that allowed for earlier parole eligibility for any prisoner who was under twenty-three at the time of the offense. At their sentencing, this program meant that Lila, who was eighteen at the time of the killings, was eligible for parole in twenty-five years instead of in the original fifty years that she had received, but Haze had been twenty-three at the time of the killings and just past the age limit. The law has since been expanded to any prisoner who was under the age of twenty-six, meaning Haze is eligible for parole in 2039. He has hope now, he said, a goal. If he keeps his head down and stays out of trouble, he could be out before his fiftieth birthday. It would help his case for release if, say, he came off as being more sympathetic than he had during the trial.

And beyond that possible ulterior motive, he was still hustling. When the trial was ongoing and he believed there was a chance he'd get out, he'd agree to an interview and, in the same breath, hint that he needed money and new camping gear for when he was free. After the sentencing, when the three were transported from Marin County Jail to their respective prisons, he would feign excitement about setting up a face-to-face visit, and then casually mention that he needed help getting in contact with Lila—something her attorney had made clear was not a good idea. In the year since he'd arrived at the Corcoran facility, I was the only visitor he'd had. Of the two people on the outside who still spoke with him on a regular basis, his mother had trouble getting approved because of her past criminal record, and the prison was a long way from his younger brother living in Washington State. Therefore, I was his only chance to hustle somebody who wasn't a fellow inmate.

I never capitulated to any of his asks, though I would sometimes treat him to an ice cream bar or a cold drink during our talks. As off-putting as his subtle cajoling was, I didn't find him to be any more dishonest than any of the many other street kids I've interviewed over the years. He and a lot of street kids I've talked to shared a trait of being deceptively deceptive, which told me less about their moral character and more about how long they had been on the streets. Because on the streets, you have to always be hustling. You have to be shrewd. You could genuinely have the best intentions and want to do something for someone, but at the same time, you must also weigh how that act would benefit you. You have to always be looking out for yourself because if you don't, nobody else will.

In any case, I corroborated—and contradicted—what I could from his account of his life and the killings with testimony from the hearings and interviews with investigators, his mother, and other people who had been in his life at some point. I caught him in outright lies several times, some just completely out of the realm of possibility. But toward the end of our talks, I began to wonder whether we could really consider a lie to be a lie if the person telling it truly believed it to be real.

Haze had enough trouble with time, memory, and some basic facts, and had ingested enough psychedelics throughout his life that he may legitimately have experienced something different from what had actually taken place. And at various points throughout his childhood, he had been diagnosed with schizoaffective disorder. "They said I couldn't differentiate reality from fantasy," he said.

He would tell me about how he and Lila, whom he referred to by her street name, Māhealani, had been forced to leave San Francisco because the city had begun clearing out homeless encampments in preparation for the Super Bowl. But reports of those sweeps didn't begin until well after they were in custody in Marin County Jail—they were arrested in October 2015, and the Super Bowl in San Francisco took place in February 2016. He described one experience he had while tripping on LSD in which he climbed a tree in San Francisco's Botanical Garden and found a bicycle waiting for him at the top, which he then rode all over the city, up and down all the hills. He may have been high at the time, but he insisted that this had all really happened. He came to with the bicycle still in his possession, but the tires were both flat, he said.

None of this makes a lie a truth. It doesn't even absolve him of his guilt. To be found not guilty by reason of insanity in the state of California, a defendant has to convince a jury that he either did not understand the nature of the act or did not understand that what he did was wrong. There was a reason why his attorneys didn't pursue this defense. Beyond the fact that it's a high threshold to prove, Haze knew exactly what he was doing at the time of Audrey's and Steve's murders. That is without question. He knew they were robbing Audrey and Steve at gunpoint, and he knew full well what would happen if something went wrong during the robbery. He may not have set out to kill them, but he admitted, "If I set myself to something, I'm the type of person that, no matter what, will do whatever it takes to get it done."

He knew what he was doing, just as he knew what he was doing when the three robbed a drug dealer at gunpoint in Golden Gate Park just before Audrey crossed into their path. He knew what he was doing as an eleven-year-old, running with other youth like him at San Diego's Ocean Beach, going into skateboard shops and grocery stores and rushing out with hundreds of dollars' worth of merchandise. He knew what he was doing each time he responded with violence when he was hitchhiking around the country, whether it was smashing a beer bottle into the face of a romantic adversary or shooting out the taillight of a man's car because he thought the man had been hitting on the girl he had been traveling with that night.

He knew what he was doing, and that is without question, because he had done it time and time before. He spoke of his misdeeds with an air of pride, laughing about crimes and acts of violence as if they were silly party anecdotes. He had trouble piecing together bits of his child-hood and remembering the years and months that events took place, but when it came to his exploits, he could recount every detail down to the number of teeth he broke when he punched a man in the face and the venti Java Chip Frappuccino with an extra shot of espresso and caramel drizzle that he bought at Starbucks the morning after Audrey's murder, using the cash he'd taken from her.

His bravado was jarring. Although he clearly understood what was a crime and what wasn't, he showed no remorse for his wrongdoings. He chuckled while telling the tale of how he and his buddies robbed a skate shop in San Diego so many times that it went out of business, of how he was sent to juvenile hall because a kid had said something bad about his mother. "I broke his face," he jeered.

Haze once told his young stepsister that he was the devil. His own father believed him to be the spawn of Satan. "Proof that evil exists," said the mother of one of his victims. But we can't discuss the concept of evil without considering the origin of it. We can't call someone a monster without analyzing how monsters are made. It's the long-fought debate of nature versus nurture, and if there's anything we can take away from Haze Lampley's life, it's that it's both.

His attorney said at his sentencing that his mother had used drugs while he was in the womb, meaning he entered this world already hooked. Though his mother, Mindi Bowman, denies that, Haze is at least the third generation on his mother's side to struggle with drugs and alcohol. "Whether I was actually on drugs or not, it is a chemical dependency that everybody in my family has," he said.

He had behavioral issues from the beginning as well. While Mindi remembered him as a happy and curious kid up until the age of seven, Haze has a specific memory of throwing one of his toys with enough force to shatter a door when he was just three or four. That was the first time someone—his grandmother—had called him crazy, he said. It wouldn't be the last time. "I was a fucked-up kid," he has admitted more than once. Later on in his childhood, a mental health professional determined that he was somewhere on the autism spectrum and was possibly manic-depressive. At a certain point in his early years, he developed a flat affect, an inability to understand or express emotions—something he still exhibits to this day.

He may have been born with a propensity toward addiction, and possibly with the sort of chemical imbalances that lead to mental illness or personality disorders, but he was also born into a life of crime, violence, and drug use—a life that he remained steeped in pretty much until his arrest in 2015. His first memory is as a toddler, slipping off the side of a crevasse in the Santa Cruz Mountains, where he, his younger half brother, his mother, and her boyfriend were hiding out because the authorities were after the boyfriend for manufacturing LSD. His grandfather used to slip a shot of whiskey into his bottle to get him to fall asleep. And while he loves his mother and will never say a bad word against her, she was using through most of his childhood and getting involved with men with violent tendencies. One boyfriend would regularly beat him, his mother, and his younger brother, and would sometimes lock him and his brother in their tiny, closet-size room for no reason at all. And he and Mindi have both said that the abuse he sustained during the years that his father took custody of him irrevocably changed who he was.

"Youth growing up in situations where there is violence, whether it's witnessing it happen to someone they love or experiencing it themselves, it's just too much," said Doug Styles, the executive director of San Francisco's Huckleberry Youth Programs. "Trauma and significant trauma alter the functioning of the brain, and the more instances there are and the more severe they are, you are actually changing the physiology of people."

All this is only exacerbated by drug use, and without proper mental health treatment, the drugs become both a crutch to help cope with the madness inside and the fuel that makes that already-unpredictable inferno burn fiercer. Mix that all together and toss it onto the streets, where your existence is just one long, sleep-deprived scramble for survival, and you get Haze Lampley. You get millions of kids just like him, who remain on the streets this very day, panhandling, committing petty crimes, and just trying to stay alive in a world that either merely ignores them or outright wants them dead.

Sit down with any of them for a few minutes, and they will tell you a similar life story. They will hack that same lung-shaking cough that comes with heavy smoking and sleeping out in the cold, and they will reveal that same cagey calculation of those around them, of who will help them and who will hurt them, no matter how trusting and friendly they appear. Spend just a little time with them, and they will show you the hurts, the past traumas, that haunt them and their actions each and every day. And you will learn that while each individual is different, the way their pain has shaped their lives is tragically and frustratingly the same.

Haze had one story that he repeated to me on several occasions. Each telling contained the same core details, as if they had been etched into his brain, and each time he told it, he spoke with the shuttered pauses of someone deeply affected by the events. For what little emotion he displayed, his silences said more than anything else.

He was twelve and was running around with a crew of street kids in San Diego's Ocean Beach. He lived with his mother then, in an apartment with a stepfather and his two stepsiblings, but he spent most of his days and nights with this crew, committing petty crimes and doing drugs. His best friend was a fourteen-year-old kid named Smiley who had introduced him to this crew and this life. One night, a few blocks away on the beach, Smiley got caught in a drive-by shooting. "He took a couple rounds to the chest," Haze said. "There was nothing I could do. I just held him and cried until he was gone."

Haze has no idea what Smiley's real name was, or whether he had possibly been older than he seemed, but he was certain that it took place in San Diego, in the Ocean Beach neighborhood, somewhere between the dog beach and the pier, three streets back from the beach near Bacon Street. The San Diego Police have no record of such a crime taking place, and even if Ocean Beach were the sort of neighborhood where shootings occurred often, the killing of a teenager is something that would have registered. When I asked Haze why the police had no record of such a shooting or homicide—and whether he had possibly misremembered and the shooting had happened elsewhere—he answered that the police never responded to the scene. But in one of the later retellings, he specifically said, "I didn't let him go until the cops pried him out of my hands."

And herein lies the conundrum that is Haze Lampley. From speaking to him, I had no doubt that he'd witnessed something traumatic and violent that had affected him deeply. But I had no way of confirming whether it was this shooting that he remembered so specifically. I could not prove that he was lying, yet I felt certain that the trauma was real.

Nothing made that clearer than in the way he clung to the idea of living on his family land in Oregon, where he and Lila were heading before they bulldozed through the lives of the Carey and Carter families in October 2015. He consistently referred to this land at some point in every one of our talks, this land where he still plans to live out the rest of his days once he gets out of prison. Oregon—for him it would always be Oregon. Somewhere in his travels wandering through the country, this plot of land became more than just land to him. It was Nirvana, the promised land where all was perfect. It was the answer to the question that gnawed at him, the question he tried to ignore, the question of whether there was more to life than his current broken existence. It was a promise after a lifetime of broken promises, a promise of safety, of happiness, of something better. It was a glimmer of hope in a hopeless existence, the tiniest flicker of light in the constant darkness of endless night. It was a home. "No matter what the world has taken from me, this was mine," he told me. "This was mine and nobody could take it."

I asked each kid I spoke with what message they hoped I would convey with this book. The question always caught them off guard—so few people actually ask them what they want or what they think. When I asked Haze the same question, in that brief moment of uncertainty, I believe I saw him at his most genuine. He dropped his bravado, his mocking laugh, and grew quiet for just a beat before he answered.

"Understanding," he said. When I left the visitation room that day, I couldn't help but wonder whether he was asking that not just of the readers, but of himself as well—whether, after all this time, he still could not comprehend his own actions, or the circumstances that led him to where he is today.

TWELVE

Portland, Oregon

D inner service was not for another few hours at the St. Francis of Assisi Dining Hall in southeast Portland, but the area around the building remained crowded with overflowing carts and bicycles. A bearded man discreetly lit up a bowl as he crouched next to a repurposed stroller, while across the way, several others sat with their backs against a wall, listening to music.

Tents, tarps, and makeshift shelters spilled onto the sidewalks, and the sounds of construction on glittering luxury apartments punctuated the quiet peace and chatter around the dining hall where up to three hundred people a day can sit down to a decent meal in the basement of a Roman Catholic church. A young woman attached a brown cover over her tent with twine, her belongings strewn around her. A few feet away, a giant stuffed panda bear lay facedown over a one-person hideaway. On the other side of the block, a man chatted with another person sitting in a beat-up van, overloaded with possessions, while the soft rain that Portland residents call "mizzle" fell onto the brightly colored umbrella that provided cover for the busted window of a sedan parked two cars down.

Three years ago, it was here that the police had caught up with Haze, Lila, and Sean, just two days after the murder of Steve Carter.

As the three ate lunch in the dining hall, local police, some in tactical gear, amassed in the area, keeping watch on the stolen silver Volkswagen parked nearby.

Marin County authorities had been tracking the three through the GPS on the Carters' car. They stopped once at a gas station in Point Reyes, about sixteen miles from where Steve bled out on the trail, going first to the bathroom to wash the blood off the ripped cash they had taken from Steve's bullet-pierced wallet. Haze still had Steve's blood on his hands from going through his pockets. They continued on, stopping at a McDonald's in Grants Pass, Oregon, and to buy some weed in Roseburg.

Haze doesn't remember much of the drive north, but looking back, he wished they had ditched the car earlier. "The maximum amount of time you want to stay with a stolen car is twenty-four hours," he said. "But we were hella coming down. It was a good place to sleep. And it was raining."

Haze knew the St. Francis dining hall well, from the days he and his mother had lived on the streets of Portland with her then-boyfriend, who went by the name Bam Bam. It was shortly after he had gotten out of the group home in California, and despite the precariousness of their living situation, Haze loved this period of his life. He could roam in a way that he'd never gotten to before—he had a choice now, to be homeless on his own or homeless in the company of Mindi and Bam Bam. And they all knew where to go for services. They had friends on the streets to look out for them. They had security, in a way, in their lack of security—their community of other homeless folks had their backs. "It was the most freedom I had in my life up to that point," Haze said.

The St. Francis dining hall was a favorite haunt during this period. Whenever he needed a break from the persistent drizzle of the Pacific Northwest, he'd hide out in the dayroom to wait out the rain. Here, they could shower and enjoy warm meals, surrounded by a community of people who knew them. "I could ask anybody, 'Hey, you seen my mom?' and they'd be like, 'Oh yeah, you're Mindi and Bam Bam's kid!'" Haze said.

It had been years since Haze had called these streets his home, but when they pulled up in the stolen car of a murdered man, he expected to still find people who knew him. Haze wanted to find where Bam Bam was living and hide out with him until "the heat died down." He wanted to ditch the car and Sean, and then he and Lila would continue on to the cabin when it was safe.

Some did remember Haze. Mindi received several phone calls from friends who knew him almost immediately after the police took him into custody. A man interviewed by *The Oregonian* after the arrests recalled having seen him in the area in the spring, and one woman interviewed by the *San Francisco Chronicle* remembered him as "a good kid." She most likely did not know that his only thought when the police swarmed him, Lila, and Sean outside the dining hall was to grab the stolen gun that still had traces of Audrey's blood on it and "shoot one of the cops."

Three years after their arrest, few remain who remember the events of that day. The woman who is now the director of the dining hall, Miriam Montes, remembers hearing about it, but wasn't there when it took place. But she knows far too well about the lives that Haze, Lila, and Sean lived before they got there. It had been her life too.

Miriam grew up in Tacoma, Washington, the daughter of an alcoholic, cocaine-addicted mother. From the age of thirteen to nineteen, she cycled through forty-seven foster homes but spent most of that time running away and living on the streets.

"I had foster parents that were abusive, I had racist foster parents, I had foster parents that would let me get drunk and then let their son sleep with me," she said. "That's the part that people forget with homeless youth: when they run away and live on the streets, they run the risk of getting raped and beaten every day. Yes, it's a risk. But at least it's a risk. Sometimes at home, it's a guarantee. At home, you can guarantee that your mom or dad is going to punch you in the mouth. You know it's going to happen, and at least on the streets, you can find yourself a street family that is going to protect you and stop that from happening."

Miriam's street family taught her that she could trade sex for drugs and a place to sleep. She spent her teen years addicted to methamphetamines and working as a prostitute. "I got beat up a lot by my older boyfriends, woke up with knives to my throat," she said. "When I was on drugs, I robbed cabdrivers. I did a lot of things I wasn't proud of. It was rough and it was hard and it was horrible, and I wouldn't wish it on my worst enemy."

Miriam only got off drugs and off the streets when she got pregnant with her daughter at twenty-one—the wake-up call she needed to pull herself out of that life. Now, she spends her days advocating for those suffering through something she understands all too well, fighting her frustration over how the system has set up people born into poverty to fail. "They say go get a job," she said. "What's the first part of a job application? An address. And you need ID. How do you get ID? In Oregon, you have to have a utility bill or a lease or something to prove that you live here. If you're a homeless person in Oregon, how do you pull that off?"

She shook her head. "It's the definition of irony. There are people who are literally dying on the street because it's so cold out while two blocks away they're putting up apartments that are going to cost $1,200 for a studio. And those are the people who are going to complain because they don't want to look out their window and see a homeless person dying."

We need housing, she said. We need better policies. But most of all, Miriam said, we need more compassion.

"Most of them want to do the right thing," she said. "Most of them want to live a better life. But they can't. Once you're in that, you're so entrenched. How do you get out? We're doing triage. We're just triaging, and there's no follow-up and no aftercare. They're stuck in this vicious cycle until someone somewhere gives them that lucky break."

~

After speaking with Miriam, I made my way downtown to meet some friends for lunch. On the way, I passed a blonde woman pushing a shopping cart filled with blankets. No one else was on the street but us, and in a moment of whimsy, she hopped up on the bottom ledge of the cart to ride it like a scooter down the sidewalk. She couldn't see what I saw—one of her blankets had fallen off the side of the cart and was in danger of tangling up in the wheels. "Whoa!" I said, running over to stop her before she could wipe out. "Oh wow, thanks," she said, her eyes wide.

This was Stephanie, the thirty-one-year-old street kid who told me about her friend getting raped on the other side of the bridge. It was windy and gray the day we met, and Stephanie wore several layers of sweatshirts and sweatpants to protect herself against the cold. She had been on her way to the women's shelter for a shower when we ran into each other.

She told me she'd been on and off the streets since she'd run away from home at twelve. She'd had to run away, she said, because her brother had been molesting her and had gotten her pregnant. She'd miscarried, but didn't get the medical help she needed because her parents "were strung out on drugs."

Most of the kids I talked to sort of shrugged off the question about whether or not they wanted to get off the streets. It was a variation of the homeless-by-choice trope: Of course they're happy where they are. Of course they're living the life they want to live. Of course this was all their choice. Because what's the alternative? But Stephanie didn't pussyfoot around any of that. In a matter of minutes, she went from the whimsical girl trying to ride a shopping cart down the sidewalk to a desperate woman seeking any kind of relief.

"I've been here my whole life, and I really need to get inside," she said. "I'm sick of being out here. Something bad is going to happen to me if I don't get off these streets downtown. It's really bad down here."

She proposed rubbing dirt on my face and having me go undercover with her to the local housing office to see how difficult the process is. "The housing authorities have talked to me for years," she said. "They know me. They know I'm out here. But they're making it so I can't make a move, and the people want me to jump through their hoops and stuff. It's just impossible sometimes."

The problem lies in her shopping cart—her three shivering Chihuahua mixes, Nikita Lynn, Trixie Lou, and Whetta Jean. She's had them for ten years, since they were puppies. She calls them her babies because, in a way, they are. She's sterile after the bad miscarriage when she was a child. These tiny little dogs are all the family she has.

It's here that whatever solutions out there for the homeless get complicated. It's understandable why a housing authority won't allow animals. But to Stephanie, this point is nonnegotiable. She's cold, she's terrified, and she's sick of sleeping on the sidewalk. But she'd rather do that than give up her dogs.

"It's crazy because this is the only thing I've done for myself," she said. "My sisters have kids, and I don't have kids. I can't have kids. These are my kids."

THIRTEEN

Alyssa stood on Haight Street one sunny afternoon wearing the forlorn expression of a cartoon hangdog. Her slumped shoulders curled inward around the small cardboard sign she held with both hands; her pale eyebrows furrowed in contrition. "EBT doesn't pay for tampons," the sign read.

The seventeen-year-old had a coltlike quality about her, all gangly limbs and quiet skittishness. She wore her hair, so blonde it was almost white, pulled back in a simple knot and out of her open, freckled face. Cigarette smoke had yellowed her teeth already, but when she smiled, her blue eyes lit up in a show of innocence that seemed out of place with her reality.

I ran into Alyssa on my way to meet Christian for the first time at his brick-and-mortar location for Taking it to the Streets. It was summer again, cool and temperate, as usual in San Francisco. At the women's state prison in Chowchilla, Lila Alligood was about to turn twenty-one. Haze was about to turn twenty-six. It had been three years since the murders of Audrey and Steve—more than seven since my fateful meeting with Dave Thompson at Buena Vista Park—and in that time, generations of street kids had passed through this city, some staying and others staying for just a while. Few remember or even know of the murders that shook the community in 2015. For sure, nobody remembers a kid named Dave who had stopped by in the summer of 2011. Time moves in different ways when you live in and for the present, never looking back and never looking forward, and a year can seem like a lifetime when you're a kid, let alone a street kid. Haze, Lila, and Sean were ancient history for a kid like Alyssa. Today, she had to worry about spanging enough cash for her and her boyfriend to get food later, about setting up camp again in Buena Vista Park and staying safe from the wing nuts out there. She had to deal with the pain of a rib she'd broken just before arriving in San Francisco three weeks earlier, ignoring her quiet concerns that it had healed wrong and she'd always have this hard bump on her torso where it had once been smooth. She had to figure out how to get tampons, the good kind with the plastic applicator, not the gross cardboard ones that the free clinic offers.

She knew what she was getting into when she'd dropped out of high school in Peoria, Illinois, and followed her boyfriend to California six months earlier, she happily told me as we walked to a Walgreens on Stanyan Street so I could buy her tampons. She knew they wouldn't have a place to stay, nor would they have jobs or a way to make steady money, and still, she'd scrimped and saved up enough from her part-time job at Walmart to buy a $155 Greyhound bus ticket to join her boyfriend in Venice Beach. "I knew it was going to be that way, but I'd go through thick and thin with him," she said. "I love him. I'd do anything for him, and with him."

She'd spent her childhood bouncing from relative to relative around Illinois, with her mother fighting a drug addiction and her father in and out of prison on drug charges. She was closest to her mother's father, who had raised her until the age of eleven, but she clashed with her grandmother. "She put me down a lot," Alyssa said over a cheeseburger I bought her at Burger Urge on Haight Street. "I can't say it wasn't my fault, because I was a pretty bratty child. I didn't have my mom, I didn't have my dad, and I was like, 'Where are they? Why don't I get letters or calls from them?' It made me really upset, and I'd act out because of it. And my grandma, she'd be like, 'Go to your room,' and I'm not allowed to leave my room for like forever, and I had to eat dinner up there and everything. I hated it."

But beyond the typical behavioral issues of a confused child, Alyssa suffered from depression and anxiety, and had "freak out" episodes of self-harm—all of which her family was ill-equipped to handle. She moved back in with her mother when she was eleven, and within a year, she was hospitalized. Her mother sent her to live with an overly religious aunt and uncle, and "I went to the hospital like five times when I was there," Alyssa said. She returned to her mother, and then to her father, following his release from prison, and then back with her mom before she decided to follow her boyfriend to California. By then, the grandfather she loved had died. There was nothing tying her to Illinois anymore, but out west, there was her boyfriend.

"I've been in Illinois my whole life," she said, taking care not to talk with her mouth full of burger. "I've never really been out of state. Illinois is one of those places where, if you don't get out, you're probably going to be stuck there forever. It's just that shitty a place."

California was new and different, she said, and the weather was great and the people interesting. But even just a few months in, living on the streets wears on a person, and Alyssa was feeling it. "My body hurts," she said. "It hurts all the time from carrying all my stuff around and sleeping on the ground." After the skateboarding accident that had led to her broken rib, she'd gone to the Cole Street Youth Clinic at the Huckleberry Youth Health Center "because it's free and all that," and they realized she had a lung infection on top of the broken rib. "Every time I coughed, it hurt so bad," she said. "They gave me Motrin, and they gave me some cough medicine to help with the cough and pain." Because of the pain, she couldn't carry her full pack with her at all times, so she'd hidden it in Golden Gate Park, from where it was promptly stolen.

When I spoke with Alyssa, it had been more than a month since she'd slept in a bed, and the last bed she'd slept in was actually just an old IKEA mattress that she and her boyfriend had found abandoned in Southern California. At most, she got about five hours a night—she and her boyfriend had to make sure to pack up their tent before the police came by to hassle them in the morning—and though Buena Vista felt safer than Golden Gate Park, it was hard to relax not knowing exactly what else was out there.

But she liked the street kid community in San Francisco. Even though strangers more readily gave her and other panhandlers cash in Southern California, "There's a lot more love here in San Francisco than in LA," she said. "A lot more love. There are a lot of sketchy, shitty people in LA, shady people who will pretend to be your friend and then screw you over. But like, the other homeless people here, you know. They're not sketchy or mean. There are some who are sketchy and mean, but if you're going to be that way, you'll definitely get kicked off of Haight Street."

~

Seven years had passed since I met Dave in Buena Vista Park, and in those seven years, the rose tint on the way I viewed the world of street kids had worn off. As I sat at a small corner table at Burger Urge with Alyssa, listening to her animated chatter about her life and plans, I thought of how Haze had said he had been so desensitized to violence that he could watch a young woman get shot in the head and continue on, completely unfazed. Alyssa had a sweetness about her that is rare these days when it comes to teenage girls, and speaking with her after spending hours in a prison visiting room with Haze felt like walking outside on the first day of spring. I wondered whether, one day, those clear blue eyes that looked up at me so earnestly over her burger would deaden like Haze's, whether they would one day stare out blankly as if nothing reached them. I wondered whether, one day, this emotive girl would witness or experience enough violence that she too could walk away from bloodshed without a second thought. I was maybe twelve years older than this girl sitting in front of me, and I felt every single one of those years, heavy and unwieldy, stretching out across the small table that separated us.

After spending the afternoon with her, I left thinking she was a good kid with good intentions. Like all street kids, she smoked weed and cigarettes, but she told me she had no plans to fall down the rabbit hole of hard drugs, given her family's history of addiction. Whenever she talks to her mother over Facebook chat, her mother makes a point to emphasize that hard drugs need to be a "not even once" sort of thing for her, and after seeing what they did to her parents, Alyssa told me she has no desire to try them. But with her anxiety and depression, weed can only do so much. Sometimes her anxiety is so bad she can barely bring herself to leave the tent in the morning, but she has to make sure they're all packed up before the police arrive. She longs for the antianxiety medication she had when she was receiving consistent mental health treatment, but getting a prescription and the care she needs is difficult even for those with steady health care, resources, and a support network. There are days when it's tempting, she admitted, to try a stronger form of self-medication.

But all in all, Alyssa is confident that her homelessness is temporary. "I know this one guy in Venice," she said, her eyes wide. "He's been homeless for years and years and hasn't heard from his wife, his kids, nothing. He's an alcoholic now, and he's so depressed and bitter, and it's really sad." That won't ever happen to her, Alyssa said. She has her eighteen-year-old boyfriend, Zared, a good-looking boy with a thick swath of dark hair and a skateboard constantly tucked under his arm. He had just skated up to Alyssa when I approached her on the street.

I offered to go with her to buy some tampons, and she looked to him before she answered. He asked whether that was what she wanted. She nodded, and they kissed tenderly before we departed. "Me and him, we keep each other in check," she said. "As long as I have him, I feel like we'll be OK."

They started dating during her freshman year of high school—they had both been skipping class when they met in the hallway—and they stayed together even when she changed schools and he eventually took off for the West Coast. Alyssa believed he left for California about a year ago, when he was seventeen, because there was a warrant out for him for a marijuana-related offense, and he told her that "weed's legal here and he can't get in trouble for it and California won't extradite," she said. I ran a quick Google search on him, and found only an old missing person report out for him when he was fifteen.

Zared seemed like a good kid too, and in the few seconds I saw him and Alyssa together, I believed there was genuine affection between them. I believed that they did actually keep each other in check, and that as long as they had each other, they could be happy, no matter the circumstances. But so much can go wrong when your whole world revolves around a teenage boy, and like so many teenage girls in the throes of their first romance, Alyssa hung the moon upon his neck and believed that the stars that filled her eyes when she looked at him meant that they were meant to be. She never called him by name, and referred to him only as "him," as if there were no other "hims" in this world. She admitted that she did most of the spanging for the two of them because she just makes more money than he does and she would rather do the work than not get to spend any time with him. And when I asked her what she wanted at Burger Urge, she slyly requested two cheeseburgers, saying she was really hungry, though I doubted that this wisp of a girl had ever eaten two cheeseburgers in one sitting before in her life. She ended up packing up the second burger to bring back to

Zared. I had offered at the beginning of our afternoon together to get him something to go, and she made the shrewd decision to make sure I would follow through.

They were in San Francisco because Zared had friends in San Francisco. They were maybe thinking of going to Mississippi so he could reconnect with his estranged father. They have no set plans, and no idea of what's to come beyond what's right in front of them—a terrifying prospect for any person in any circumstance, but Alyssa said she's not scared. "Because I have him," she said. "If I didn't have him, I'd probably go home. I'd definitely go home. That's what I tell him, I tell him if we ever break up, I'm going to go home."

I paused for a beat before asking whether she had the money to get back to Illinois if she had to, or whether she had enough to care for herself before she could find a way home—she and Zared currently share a tent, and he carried most of their shared belongings after her backpack was stolen. "Probably not," Alyssa shrugged. "I'd probably have to spange up for a bus ticket, and that would probably take a whole week. I only get like twenty bucks a day maybe, and I spange from like noon to five o'clock. Sometimes I get less than twenty bucks."

So much can go wrong when you're a teenage girl, let alone a teenage girl without a stable place of residence. But in this moment in time, their homelessness was an adventure. "I just want to see more," Alyssa said. "Since I've been out of Illinois, I've met so many cool people, and I've done so much stuff that I wouldn't think I would ever do in my whole entire life. Just imagine what else is out there, what kind of people are out there, you know? There's just so many things out there that are there for me to discover."

One day she'll get her GED. One day she'll rejoin what most consider "normal" society, and get a job and a home and some stability. She dreams of becoming an artist, and Zared wants to be a DJ, but beyond that, they haven't thought much beyond their day-to-day.

One day they'll settle down and get an apartment and start a family, Alyssa said. "But right now, I'm only seventeen," she said. "He's eighteen. We have our whole lives."

She asked for the time, and, upon realizing that it was later than she'd meant to stay, jumped up to grab a to-go box and gather up her belongings. I gave her my phone number, just in case, and she told me to contact her on Facebook—she has an old smartphone, she explained, but no cellular plan, so Facebook is the only way she can stay in touch.

"I hope everything works out for you guys," I said as she headed out the door.

"I think it will." She smiled. "I have a good feeling."

FOURTEEN

The Road from Here

Something I don't think a lot of journalists are willing to acknowledge is that while we strive to go into our interviews with an open mind and a blank-slate attitude, with certain subjects, we know what we want them to say. Anyone who claims otherwise is lying to you, because as hard as we fight it, we're still human beings who abide by the same societal contract and have the same expectations of behavior as everybody else. We'll try to coax out the answers we want by rephrasing our questions or displaying sympathy when we have none, but in the end, what separates the good reporters from the hacks are their actions when those expectations are not met.

I didn't come to terms with this until after maybe my fourth sit-down with Haze. Going into those interviews, I knew they would be hard and that the details of his life would be disturbing. I had prepared for that. But it wasn't until I got in my rental car with its sickly sweet rental-car smell and started on the mind-numbing four-hour drive back to San Francisco that I realized that what I'd wanted from him was remorse—and I never got it.

I arrived in Corcoran hoping to find a tormented and repentant man in the throes of mental self-flagellation, haunted by the lives he'd taken and the families he'd hurt. I wanted him to see Lokita Carter's tears when he closed his eyes and hear Isabelle Tremblay's words in his moments of quiet. I wanted the impact statements read at his sentencing to follow him for the rest of his days. "Three people killed my dad, for what? A little cash? A car?" sobbed Emily Hansen, Steve's daughter. "He wasn't there to walk me down the aisle at my wedding. When I have kids, they will never be able to know their grandfather. And how do I tell them how he died?"

Of the three, Lila was the only one who addressed the victims' families herself, while Sean's and Haze's attorneys read the statements that they had prepared earlier. "I'm so sorry for what I did, the decisions I made, and the indescribable pain I've caused others," Lila said in her girlish, shaking voice, her nose still red from the tears she'd shed, while David Brown, Haze's attorney, rushed through Haze's statement in an emotionless, to-the-point manner. "I know that what I've done has devastated so many," Brown read. "I wish I could go back in time and change things. I know I cannot ask for your forgiveness, but I hope you find peace someday."

I wanted more from Haze. I wanted to hear it from him, the pretty words of guilt and anguish, of the pain he knew he'd caused. But when I pushed him on his reaction to the sentencing and the victim impact statements, he just shrugged. "I can't remember most of it," he said.

I shouldn't have been surprised. When I spoke with him in Marin County Jail, it had been right after Lokita Carter took the stand to set the stage for the preliminary hearing. She walked before the people who had taken her love from her, with a strength and grace that I still think of to this day, and looked into each of their faces. I asked Haze whether that was difficult for him. "It wasn't as hard as most people would think it would be," Haze said.

On the drive back that day, I realized the true source of the nausea that I had attributed to nerves and car sickness. It was a new sensation for me. As a journalist specializing in crime and criminal justice,

I've come in contact with a fair number of people that most would consider repugnant—convicted murderers, gang members, sexual abusers of adults and children, corrupt authority figures, and worse—and I've always prided myself in setting aside any preconceived notions or biases and giving them fair coverage by looking at their humanity. But I couldn't find that in Haze, in how detached and apathetic he seemed when it came to the harm he had done. I had almost begged him for some kind of reaction to the murder of Audrey Carey, and got nothing. Later, after more prodding, he admitted that "the old dude kind of fucked with me." I pounced on that tidbit, pushing to get him to own up to some remorse for the murder of Steve Carter. But that led nowhere, with his improbable tale of accidentally emptying the entire clip of a fully functioning semiautomatic handgun that had no sort of modifications, a move that would have required somebody actively pulling the trigger multiple times. "If it had been intentional, it wouldn't have weighed on me," he said—meaning he went into an armed robbery knowing full well that if something went awry, he would have to take a life, and he was OK with that. Just before the shooting, as he got fed up with Lila and Sean arguing about who would do it, he said he told them that they had to figure it out because it would only end badly if it fell to him. "You guys know how I am," he'd told them. Haze admitted that he assumed that Steve would know how to disarm a person and fight back. Without question, Haze said, "I would have shot him if he tried something."

The only regret of his that I believed to be real was that Steve's dog Coco had gotten hit in the shooting and lost an eye. "I've been abused by humans my whole life," he said. "People who have been abused, we connect with animals who have been abused. I'm never going to get over the fact that Coco got shot in all that." Other than that, my impression was that even though Steve's murder gave him pause, he was more upset that it was his actions with Steve that led to them getting caught. "It's only because of him and that car that we got arrested," he said.

"I could have lived with my conscience of witnessing a murder," he said. "I've been through quite a few of those. But I don't really know anymore."

Mindi has never met Lila, Haze's purported great love, but she holds little respect for her and can't understand why Haze is still trying to get in touch with her after three years apart. "I know if she could have, she would have pinned everything on my son," she said. "And I don't think highly of people that would turn their back on somebody that they say they love. Like, 'Oh, I didn't really have anything to do with this situation. If it wasn't for him being abusive, coercing me into something I didn't want to do . . .' She was fully there and willing to do whatever as well."

But where mother and son diverge in opinion there, everywhere else they remain two beings shaped from the same mold, particularly when it comes to the killings. Haze maintained that he never would have done what he did if he had been "in the right mind," though what that means for someone who has been abusing drugs since childhood is still unclear. Mindi shares that viewpoint. "Anybody in addiction can do anything because when you're high, you're not who you really are," she said. "Things can happen, and things can get out of control really fast when you're high. If my son was clean and maybe just smoking some weed, I wouldn't think he could do what he was accused of. I don't think he would have been in a situation where it would have come to that. But anything is possible when drugs and alcohol are involved." These days, Mindi goes out of her way to counsel any street kids she runs into, giving them beanies and gloves and hand warmers. "I communicate with them where my son is at because of the choices that he made and that things can change really quick, in hopes that maybe another kid won't make those same choices, or might think for a split second that, hey, wait a minute, my whole life depends on this choice," she said. The impression I got was that the choice she referred to had less to do with firing a gun at two complete strangers and more to do with using drugs.

This was definitely a shared trait of theirs, this need to detach themselves from their actions and talk about their lives as if they hadn't been the ones to live them out. It's a trait that becomes really unsettling when they talk about the killings. Part of it is they both seem to be of the mentality that what's happened has happened and it does no good to dwell on the past. Both of them rarely mention the victims in all this, or the victims' families, or any sort of emotion they may feel toward the victims and the families. They cannot seem to acknowledge that the Carey and Carter families will suffer through a lifetime of unfathomable grief because of the senseless actions of Haze and his cohorts; instead, they seem to see it in terms of how it pertains to them and their lives.

"The Creator has his way of doing things," Mindi said. "We all have choices to make, and when you make bad choices, certain things happen. That's just the way of the Creator. Now Haze is over a year clean. I would much rather him not be where he's at, but at least I know he's OK."

On the one hand, I can understand and even appreciate this perspective of finding the positive in a purely shit situation, but on the other, it feels so utterly callous. They are weighing a tragedy directly caused by Haze against how it could actually benefit him. Two people died, but at least now Haze is sober. Sean said something similar to me as well: "I can definitely say that my outlook on life right now is completely one-eighty. Unfortunately it needed to come down to this, but I'm looking at this as a reality check. I didn't complete my education. I didn't have any goals in life but just traveling. Now I'm able to step back. This is probably what I needed to take a step back really quick and finish my education and figure out what I wanted to do with my life." If we flip the script here, he is saying that murdering someone is what he needed to get his life together.

But I've seen other kids shrug off their own tragedies in this sort of way, as just something that happened, either to them or to somebody else, and something from which they need to move forward. I thought of Momo, who straight-up said, "I'm really happy that everything fucked-up in my life happened to me. I know a lot of other women would be a lot more broken. A lot of other women would not be able to handle it." Haze told me something similar: "I'm a better person because of what I suffered," he said. "I've had hella hard-core killers tell me, 'Look, man, I couldn't have gone through half of what you've been through and survive.'

"I had the best life I could have possibly had, on my own and on drugs," Haze said. "Even when every now and then I would get too strung out."

What's happened has happened, whether by their own hand or because of someone else. For street kids, they can either see it as a boon or let it drag them down. "It is what it is," Haze said. Had his life and traumas been any different, "I wouldn't be me."

Stripped of societal niceties and general expectations of decent human behavior, this mentality is our survival instincts at their basest. Retrospection is a luxury. Compassion is a privilege. And remorse, the ability to feel guilt, to take responsibility for your misdeeds? A suicide mission, a death wish, quicksand in the fight to survive.

~

I went into these interviews with Haze hoping to shine a light on the precarious lives of street kids in hopes that they can get the help they need, so that nobody will again end up in the situation where Haze, Lila, and Sean found themselves in October 2015. That maybe with some compassion and awareness, we could end this cycle of hurt kids hurting others because that is all they know. According to Christian Garmisa-Calinsky, the former street kid who founded the nonprofit on Haight Street, nobody is ever too far gone—no one is ever too far beyond the scope of compassion that they can't be reunited with their humanity. But then we have the kids who did not get that help in time.

We have Haze, Lila, and Sean, biding their time behind bars before they rejoin society—if ever they do.

"You take away the meth, you take away some of the trauma that they had, these kids—they were kids," Christian said. "And now they're gone forever. They were already thrown away, and now they're really thrown away."

The first reaction from every street kid and former street kid I spoke with was to distance themselves from the actions of Haze, Lila, and Sean—an understandable move, considering how Haight Street residents jumped to dismiss them all as potential violent killers after the murders. But over time, some of the former street kids acknowledged that they could see how Haze, Lila, and Sean could have gotten to such a place where they felt they had to kill, especially under the influence of drugs.

"When I was on meth, I hallucinated bubble dinosaurs," Miriam Montes said. "I ripped an IV out of my arm. I went batshit crazy and woke up strapped to a bed because I was a biter. When you're on meth, it's not you anymore. You are being controlled by that drug."

Gary McCoy, the homeless outreach worker in San Francisco, can still remember the fleeting and terrifying "crazy thoughts" that would pop into his head at the height of his addiction. "I didn't act on them, but I can't imagine five or ten years of that kind of lifestyle," he said. "I know people who didn't use meth at all but by a third or fourth time, they were already hearing voices. And it just gets worse over time."

But it goes beyond drug use. The paranoia that comes with meth is always there for street kids, with or without the drug itself. They can't ever relax, not even to sleep. They have to keep moving before the cops show up or some business owner complains about them, shooing them off their sidewalks as if they were no better than the pigeons and vermin flocking among the garbage.

Within their own communities as well, they have to always assume that somebody is about to hurt them and take their things, that at any minute there will be violence or worse. Christian said some of the kids he works with are afraid to close the door while they shower when they first get into the program, knowing that that is when they are at their most vulnerable—naked, weaponless, and stripped of their belongings—that anybody can make off with the backpacks that carry their entire lives if they dare to relax for just one minute and enjoy the hot water washing the weeks of grime off them.

"I remember even three weeks in at treatment, a counselor asked me, 'When are you going to stop wearing your shoes to bed at night?'" Gary said. "I would just go to sleep fully dressed with my shoes on and my bag up every night because I felt like I had to leave at any time. I always felt like I had to go.

"It's definitely survival mode. When I was using meth, on the street with my backpack and using meth and hooking up with random people, I would never take my pants off. I would never take my pants off because everything important was in my backpack and everything more important was in my pants. I had to either be able to know where it was at or be able to leave if I had to leave. And it just gets worse and worse."

Survival is not a concept most of us operating within the confines of everyday society even consider. We live in a world where we can feed ourselves with food stocked in stores, drink water from the tap, and keep ourselves warm when night falls. We know we will never run out of toilet paper or toothpaste. "Survival" may mean enduring a soporific business meeting or emerging from gridlock traffic. But for the kids we pass every day on the street, it is their day-to-day. We can live, but they can only survive. And we hate them for it. We criminalize their existence, making it illegal for them to sit or sleep or be. We donate our money to soup kitchens and homeless charities, but complain when we see someone panhandling in front of our establishments or using a public restroom. We send them the same message over and over again that they are not welcome. Their existence is a nuisance. Their humanity is no longer.

"I was working with a student who was homeless, after her family was gentrified out of their home in Park Slope [in Brooklyn]," said Michael Niman, the expert on the Rainbows. "It took a very long time to get her to stop apologizing for existing in any space. She would apologize for the chair she was sitting in and offer it to someone else when they walked into the office. She would apologize for taking up space in a classroom, even though she was paying for that class with loans. She had internalized the trauma of couch surfing in New York City."

The factors that drive kids into the streets are legion, and every kid's story is unique. We could talk about fixing a foster care system that seems to forget about way too many kids who age out and have nowhere to go. We could talk about putting in place better drug treatment programs and providing better mental health care. But the more we go into it, the farther we spiral into a pit of hopelessness, because the fact is, too many of the systems we have in place now are broken. Even if we had the commitment and the compassion to fix them all, it would take several generations before we saw any sort of results. Beyond that, there are just some root causes of youth homelessness that we won't ever be able to fix. As long as there are children in this world, there will be parents and other adults who neglect them, abuse them, mistreat them, and molest them. Try as we might, we can't always intervene before it reaches the point of no return for the kids affected. We can't save everyone.

We can't prevent youth homelessness—not the way we approach it at present, anyway—so our only option is to treat it. The reasons behind every kid's homelessness may differ, but their experiences on the streets are the same in the end. After that first burst of freedom and escape, their lives become one prolonged dehumanizing fight for survival, and with each day spent on the streets, they drift farther and farther away from being able to leave this existence when they come to the decision to do so. In too many cases, this also means they drift farther and farther from the bulwarks of humanity that we who do not have to worry about survival accept as assumptions: compassion, empathy, a sense that a system is in place and that it will guarantee order in our lives.

We can't prevent it from happening, but once it does, we can help the kids in need. It's a Sisyphean task—for every youth that advocates like Christian and Gary and Miriam and Doug get into a place of stability, there's another kid to take his place in the streets. On top of that, there's just the cruel reality that few people care enough to spare the resources needed to help these kids. In August 2018, after four years of operation and hundreds of kids counseled and housed, San Francisco pulled the funding for Christian's nonprofit, Taking it to the Streets. It was a heartbreaking loss to the Haight-Ashbury neighborhood, where Christian and his kids had just established their footing, where the local business owners knew them and went out of their way to set aside some of their profits for the program. When I'd met Alyssa just one month earlier, she had asked me, completely out of the blue, "Have you heard of TITTS House?"—a reference to the nonprofit's tongue-in-cheek acronym. How far Christian had come, I remember thinking. I joked with him about it later, teasing him about building up such a reputation that street kids from all over the country now knew about his program. "Famous," he laughed. "Dirty kid mansion." These kids had a place, and just like that, it was gone.

~

Where Haze Lampley fits into all this is harder to answer. Right now, everything he does goes toward making sure he gets released on parole in 2039. He's taking classes for his GED and plans on getting a caregiver job for the prisoners with disabilities after that. He said he's on the waiting list for Narcotics Anonymous and has been sober since he was arrested in October 2015, though I have no way to corroborate that. He went out of his way to tell me he knows he can get drugs, even in a prison that specializes in substance abuse treatment, but he refuses to spend the money his mother sends him on that.

On paper, it appears that he's doing well for himself and staying out of trouble. But when I asked him why he was doing all this, he didn't say it was because he wanted to better himself or actually live without drugs. He has a singular focus, and that is to get out as soon as he can.

One of the detectives who built the case against the three admitted to me that he's kept awake some nights worrying about the day Haze is released on parole. While he has doubts about Sean and Lila, the detective said he can't be certain that Haze would not kill again. In a way, it's in our interest, the interest of public safety, that somebody like Haze can come back from all the horrendous trauma he both inflicted and had inflicted upon himself in the twenty-some years he's been alive—that somebody seemingly so irredeemable can be redeemed. But beyond the implications of his possible parole, Haze has children, a son and a daughter. His two biological children are both seven, with different mothers he met while traveling. Already, his son is exhibiting signs that he may suffer from the same sort of behavioral and mental health issues that Haze had growing up. When he was five, he threw such a tantrum that he broke his teacher's arm. "His mother says he's possessed by a demon," Haze said.

I brought up the question of nature versus nurture, and Haze seemed almost helpless for the first time in all our conversations. So much of his life was shaped by the trauma and pain that happened to him, yet so much feels as if it were inevitable as well; disaster and despair are in his DNA. If his children grow up in a more stable, loving environment than he did, will that be enough to keep them from being like him? "One good thing about me being in here," he said sardonically, "is that I beat the cycle of beating my kids."

Haze's father called Haze the "spawn of Satan," something that Haze eventually believed enough to start identifying himself as the devil. And now here comes his son, the next generation, possessed by a demon. "I'm scared shitless about him," Haze admitted.

We can trace back every decision and act in Haze's life to the trauma and abuse he suffered, to the predisposition to addiction and mental illness into which he was born. But that doesn't absolve him of wrong-doing. Haze knows the difference between right and wrong. He knew exactly what he was doing. We can't pretend that Haze was a hapless bystander. At some point, we need to acknowledge that he held some agency as well: that he had a choice, and he chose to kill two people. There are millions of kids just like him wandering the country today, but there are not millions of murderers, forced into committing the unspeakable by their upbringings and bloodlines.

"Smalls deserves what he gets," Haze said. "I deserve what I get. Māhealani deserves what she gets. We went through some shit. We need to accept it. Once you accept something, it's time to move on." Once again, he speaks of the murders as something that happened, not something he did. He made a choice then, and he chose bloodshed. But he has a choice to make now, and the path he chooses will make all the difference in determining the type of man he will be when he walks out those prison doors.

I once asked Haze how he spent his time in prison, and he listed off the evening lineup on the basic cable channels as if he were reading off a *TV Guide*. "I spend as much of my time as I can ignoring reality," he admitted. When I pushed about Isabelle Tremblay, Lokita Carter—the families of Audrey and Steve—he said he tries not to think of them. "That is just more emotional pain that I don't want to deal with," he said. "I try not to spend much time thinking of anything."

I saw then, in his lack of remorse, not merely the unfeeling monster that people believed him to be, but a scared boy, shaking and trying not to cry as he hid under the covers. Haze Lampley was still trying to survive. Hundreds of miles away from the streets that had hardened him, he was still that homeless kid, scrapping and fighting and stealing to stay alive. He was still that kid who snorted his first bump of heroin at the age of ten, desperate to calm the tempest of emotions roaring inside him.

Looking back, I could see it in every street kid I spoke with who steals and robs and hurts and wastes away the day doing drugs. To survive as they do means losing the last of their humanity. On the streets, emotion is an extravagance that they cannot afford. If they allowed themselves to feel bad, they wouldn't be able to do the things they need to do in order to live. It's why we abhor this particular subset of the homeless population. We detest them because they are forced to operate outside our social norms of decent human behavior. We hate them because they survive in spite of their humanity. We hate them because they are us, at our basest, stripped of all we have holding us up as a society of human beings.

Even when it came to Lila, the purported love of his life, Haze had to be pragmatic. He told me he would wait for her, and he believed she would wait for him. He didn't doubt the love and the past that they shared. But he had to be prepared for a future in which she would not feel the same way. "I want her to be in my life," he said. "I'm going to try. That's all I can do. If not, well, she'll understand. I'll find someone else to occupy my time with. I may never love someone like I love her again, but that's not the point. Man needs companionship, and that's it."

It takes time to move beyond this pragmatism, this survival mindset. While I was still mulling over the unrepentant man I saw in Corcoran, I happened upon an opportunity to meet a group of former prisoners who'd gone through a training program at Folsom State Prison that helps inmates look inward and break through to their emotions. One man, Rick Misener, a former member of the Aryan Brotherhood who had been serving a life sentence for killing a Marine, said it's almost instinctual for those with blood on their hands to hide from the truth of what they've done. "Most people don't want to own what they've done because the weight of it is too much and they don't know how to do the work," Rick said.

It took Rick twenty years—and this intensive training and support group—before he could come to terms with what he'd done. And it almost killed him to acknowledge the magnitude of his crimes—that it wasn't just one life he'd taken, but a family he'd torn apart. "How many generations have been born that don't get to know him?" he asked.

Rob Allbee, who cofounded this program—Inside Circle—likes to tell a story he heard while he was in Burkina Faso when asked about the capacity for redemption. "My friend told me that many, many centuries ago, there had been a murder in the village," Rob said. "One man had killed another man. And the way that they dealt with it was they waited a year and then they did everything they could—they call it singing you back to your medicine. With each baby that's born, while the mother is pregnant, they use those nine months to come up with a song that is just for that kid. They are sung that song their whole life, and it's a reminder of their gift. They spent a whole year trying to sing that person back to their gift, and at the end of the year, there's a big ritual at the river and they take the person down there and tie him up and put him in the canoe. A couple of people take him out to the middle of the river and throw him overboard. And the only people who can save him are the members of the victim's immediate family."

Rob asked his friend whether the family jumped into the river, whether the man had been saved—whether there was a chance for a killer to be saved. "He was always doing this," he laughed. "I asked him, 'Did they go out there?' He said, 'Choose. Choose. The human experience is you get to choose.'" It's up to us, he's saying. We can choose whether a killer can be saved.

I told Rob about Haze and my concerns over his lack of remorse. I admitted to him that I felt sick talking to Haze. And Rob told me I would have felt pretty sick talking to him forty years or so ago. Rob spent five years in prison for his friend's death. When he was seventeen, he and his best friend were committing a commercial burglary, and his friend was fatally shot by a police officer. Because his friend died in the commission of a felony, Rob was charged with his murder.

"I was so full of rage when I got out that we literally went and stole weapons," Rob said. "We were seriously going to torture and kill this guy. We were going to kidnap the cop and torture him over the phone so the police could hear us doing it and then just wait for cops to show up and take out as many as we could. That was where my head was at. I just did not give a fuck.

"So I remember that space of apathy," he said, "I remember being in that spot. That's what's happening for (Haze) now, but I still have to have faith in the human spirit enough that given the right circumstances, given the right opportunities, given an example that might come into his life, maybe that person too can eventually find some measure of health, purpose, that they matter to someone, that other people matter to him. I just have to hold out that possibility. The reality of it? Not really big. But the hope? I can't say it's hopeless. I've sat in that spot where it looked pretty fucking hopeless. All I spouted was rage.

"Inside of each human being, I really believe that down there, there's still an ember burning barely, just struggling to stay alive, just a little flicker," Rob said. "Sometimes all we have to do is fan it a little bit and it will rise."

~

Sometime after my last sit-down with Haze, I thought of Dave Thompson again, the first street kid I ever met. As I'd done every so often throughout the years since I found him in Buena Vista Park, I wondered how he was doing and whether he was still living on the streets.

I remembered joking with him about his last name when he balked at disclosing it. "'David Thompson' is generic enough that nobody will know it's you," I pointed out. Seven years later, that statement came back to haunt me. When I decided to take action this time around and find him, I realized early on that I was staring down the barrel of an impossible task. I ran the typical people searches in public databases and came up with more than three thousand results on Nexis alone. When I narrowed down the search to his home state—he told me he'd grown up in the Detroit area—I still came up with more than three thousand results. When I narrowed that down to Dave Thompsons in his age range, I found 415 possibilities. But there's a chance Dave never had a steady place of residence in his adult life. Like Haze, there's a chance he never had an identification card, or a mailing address, or anything actually tying him to a location. I ran a search on Haze and came up with twenty-nine possibilities, all of which were not him and made me pessimistic about the chances that one of the 415 results would end up being Dave.

I put out missives in traveler and dirty kid groups and talked to some homeless outreach teams about whether they knew anybody fitting his description—"He had a dog named Chicken," I told them—and I got no bites. Soon I found myself scrolling through Facebook, looking at the pages of random David Thompsons and considering whether any of them could possibly be him. I messaged one man I thought was a sure thing—they shared the same coloring and long gaunt face. I zoomed in on the photos to see whether I could spot the scar on his cheek or the tattered earlobe, but nothing was clear enough to make that determination.

This David was a video effects editor in Southern California, and for a second I let myself imagine the David Thompson I met all those years ago in this life, finding success in something he enjoyed doing. I pictured him living in a home with several roommates, going back to school, playing with Chicken at a dog park. I saw him groaning at the persistent chirp of his alarm clock in the mornings but getting up nonetheless, shuffling into the kitchen to make coffee before work. I envisioned him coming home and having a beer with his roommates in their backyard, talking and laughing deep into the night with Chicken lounging at their feet. It was such a very ordinary kind of life, yet for someone like Dave, it felt extraordinary. I liked thinking of him in this life, having found a purpose and a place in the "normie" world, but the David Thompson I messaged responded almost immediately: he was too young to be the David Thompson I wanted him to be.

I messaged a few more. "Not me. Never been to San Francisco," one David Thompson replied, and from the rest, radio silence. I started to be more judicious in whom I would message—this guy's face is too different, this one doesn't have the right hair color. It didn't take long before I found myself in a tailspin of excluding this David Thompson or that David Thompson because this one seemed too successful, this one is married and is living the perfect suburban life, this one just seems to have it too together. Some other journalists I spoke to for advice in tracking him down suggested I run criminal background checks on these David Thompsons—the unfortunate reality is that this population is more likely to be arrested for crimes, due to their visibility. I found myself engaged in a more intense version of the Facebook scrolling as I weighed the possibility of whether this or that crime could fit with the kid I'd met back then—driving under the influence, but would he have a car now? Assault—that seems possible. Public intoxication, definitely yes.

Each time I did this, I'd end up working myself into an anxious frenzy until I had to slam the lid of my laptop shut and walk away. Something about this endless pit of David Thompsons gnawed at my belly, agitating me and putting me in a dark mood. I could feel this anxiety clawing its way up my torso, stopping just before it reached my throat. There it sat, at the hollow spot where my throat met my chest, heavy and unyielding, constricting the flow of oxygen to my brain.

Finally one day, I took a deep breath and addressed this specter and realized that it was not so much a feeling but a question. Why couldn't

the Dave Thompson I met be the Dave Thompson who is now working at Google? Why couldn't he be the one with photos of his children
kissing him on the cheek? Why couldn't he have found success? Why
couldn't he have found happiness?

I thought of Christian, who'd founded a successful nonprofit and
got to rub shoulders with the mayor of San Francisco and other important politicians whom he came to meet through his work. Just a decade
ago, he was a David Thompson. Then there was Gary, the homeless
outreach worker in San Francisco. Gary has been sober since 2011,
after a friend's death made him realize that his life would end the same
way if he didn't get treatment. He got an internship with Representative
Nancy Pelosi when she was House Minority Leader, and worked for
some of the leading public officials in the city. His knowledge and
experiences are now driving policy in San Francisco, with the city rolling out pilot programs for safe injection sites based on his suggestions.
Could David Thompson have ended up like either of these men? Could
he have found his calling? Could he have a significant other waiting for
him at home, kids, friends? Could his Facebook page look like theirs,
with smiling faces and cute memories filling his life?

Then there were the other travelers I met. I thought of Sleepy,
who, like so many street kids, grew up coping with a drug-using parent. I thought of how he'd started hitchhiking to escape jail time, and
found on the road a community that loved him and accepted him and
celebrated his passions in life. He became active in the Rainbow world,
eventually counseling runaway youth who were just like he once was.
"These kids, they will figure it out eventually," he said. Maybe Dave was
living like Sleepy these days, driving around in an old van and seeing
the country, making new friends everywhere he went.

And then there was Momo. I friended her on Facebook a few
months after our first meeting, and I remember feeling surprised at
how much older she looked in her photos than she did in person. After
we met in Santa Rosa, she and Cory ambled through Arizona, Utah,

Montana, Oregon, and Idaho, where she earned money harvesting potatoes. This was her dream, she'd told me in Santa Rosa. Traveling with her little family in a bus of their own, going wherever they felt like going that day. She was houseless, but in a way, she wasn't homeless. Her home went with her.

I had asked her why she went by the street name Momo, and she said it was after the character Momoka from the Japanese anime-manga series Sgt. Frog. "She's a little fanatical and crazy," Momo said. "She has a really calm demeanor until she snaps and she goes super insane and then reverts back to normal."

"That doesn't sound like you," I said.

"I used to do that," she said. "But not anymore. I'm able to hack my brain enough." I wondered about her then, if she was hiding more of her suffering and trauma than she was willing to let on.

Perhaps, like some of the other kids I met on the road, Dave kept wandering. If this were the route Dave had taken, I would want him to be in the position of Momo or Sleepy: ambling around the country, houseless but not homeless, with people who loved and supported them with them at all times. Fulfilling a purpose by feeding others or earning money doing part-time seasonal labor. Working through whatever traumas, issues, hang-ups, or spites with each mile the wheels of their bus home ate up on the road.

Ten months after Momo and I met, she posted on Facebook that she was calling it quits. "My body can't take the road anymore," she wrote. "Mentally, I'm slipping as well. Cory has noticed me drooping and wilting as a being." She seemed to have patched up any bad blood between her and her mother after her last trip back to Spokane to recover from her surgery, and was eager to move back near her family. She and Cory mutually understood that this would mean an end to their relationship, and she wrote that they would be spending the next eight weeks "working with each other to be able to part without feeling loss." If this were the path that Dave had walked, this would be what

I'd want for him, I thought—not the part about quitting the traveling life and rejoining the "normie" life, but the ability to do so if or when the time came that he wanted to leave this life.

There's the J. R. R. Tolkien quote beloved by so many travelers and drifters: "Not all those who wander are lost." The travelers I met on the road love this saying, with many splashing it up on their Facebook pages. In my time talking to them, I came to understand that they love this quote not so much because it defends the lifestyle they chose, but because it's a nod to the fact that they are actually lost, even as they wander—and that so are the "housies" and "normies" and others who act as functioning members of society and have roots holding them firm in one place. Edie and Shay Ward, the mother and son I met in San Diego, eventually returned to Missouri, but how well they were doing remained a mystery. Edie still posted sad quotes and lyrics about her abusive late husband. It wasn't clear whether Shay was still living with her—at one point he posted about rumors that a girlfriend had kicked him out of her house. "I walked the fuck out. I chose to leave . . . All she is is manipulative," he wrote. Just a little over a week later he was in a relationship with another girl. Not all wanderers are lost, and not all who remain in one place are found.

I thought of Haze, and his fixation on the cabin in Oregon. Cabins in Oregon are not meant to be easily found. One free afternoon in Portland, I went for it, following the uphill curves of Google Maps in my rental sedan. It wasn't as bad as the drive into the Rainbow Gathering in Arizona, though each bump in the road seemed to knock just a bit more static into my radio signal until all I could hear was white-hot fuzz. The "No Trespassing" signs made me nervous, reminding me of all the times I'd been caught in the middle of nowhere covering a wildfire and having to be cognizant not to stumble into any illegal weed grows. I still had miles to go before I reached the cabin, and I no longer had cell phone service. I accidentally turned into a driveway twice, thinking it was a continuation of the road, before a pickup truck began tailing me, the very inconspicuous out-of-towner in a rental car not meant for unpaved drives. "Is this the way to the national forest?" I called out brightly, deciding that playing dumb was probably my best bet. The driver politely told me I needed to turn back around the way I came from, and I did just that, my heart thudding loudly in my ears.

Haze laughed when I relayed all this to him later. "Even I had a hard time finding my way there," he admitted. He later said it was probably a good thing I didn't actually make it to the cabin—his grandfather has a habit of shooting trespassers.

When I had asked Mindi about Haze's great dream to get to the family cabin in Oregon and start a pot farm, she had grown quiet. "Is that what he told you?" she asked.

Haze's grandfather lives up there full-time now, Mindi said, and even though it is family land, he wouldn't have tolerated having Haze living with him, especially if he was planning on growing pot. "My dad said he couldn't do that there," she said. She hinted that her father believed in living by his rules, and Haze had never liked to follow those. It never would have worked out.

After all that, it would have been for naught. This had been their destination in all this, the reason for all the bloodshed and death and destruction, but it wasn't even his at the time. It wasn't a real possibility, just a wisp of a dream slipping through their fingers. I wondered what would have happened had they made it up to the cabin. What would their next move have been, knowing this dream could not be theirs? Where would they have gone?

Haze still truly believes that is where he'll end up. Once he gets out of prison, he's going straight there, he said, and living out the rest of his days alone on that mountain. I wondered what he will do if he gets there and finds out he's not wanted, or learns that it's not what he seeks. I pictured him, his hair gray and his face lined, arriving at this piece of land and looking at what was left for him. Was the driveway as long as he remembered? The river as wide and fresh? Was all of this, any of this, worth it? Was it worth the lives of two innocent strangers? A lifetime of heartbreak for their surviving loved ones?

Not all wanderers are lost, but they are all searching for something. In the end, I realized that all so many of us are searching for, especially those who have been forced to wander for so long, is our proverbial cabin in Oregon. A place of our own. A place where we are safe. A place where we can be, where we can rest. A place that no one can take.

A cabin in Oregon is no Valhalla, no panacea for all the hurt that life has bestowed on these kids. But in moments of quiet, I like to imagine Dave arriving at his proverbial cabin, still dragging his pack and sleeping bag behind him. Maybe it's in Michigan, where he said he'd grown up. Or maybe, like Haze's cabin, it's in the Pacific Northwest, where he had been heading that day we met in San Francisco. No matter where it is, it's far from the violence and the drugs and the noise and all the people with the potential to hurt him. I see him pausing at the riverbank to wash his face and take a quick drink from his cupped hands. He leans back on his heels, soaking in the birdsong, the rustle of the wind in the trees, the sounds of the water bubbling next to him. And he stays.

ACKNOWLEDGMENTS

First and foremost, to the families of Audrey Carey and Steve Carter: Please know that this book is not offered as an excuse. There is no excuse. This is an attempt to understand why and how we got here so that no family will ever again have to experience the pain that you have suffered. I hope that this book does the memories of Audrey and Steve justice.

To everyone who took the time to share their stories with me: thank you. I asked you to reopen your wounds so that I could understand them, and you did so knowing how painful it would be. I am better for having heard your stories, and for that, I am forever grateful.

Thank you to my agent, Travis Pennington, for taking a chance on me, and a very special thanks to my editor, Carmen Johnson, and the team at Little A, for having the patience and kindness necessary for a particularly neurotic first-time author.

Thank you to my former editors and colleagues at the *San Francisco Chronicle*: I am the writer and reporter I am today because of my years at 901 Mission Street.

Thank you to my dear friends Katie Mau and Kale Williams, for letting me crash at your homes while I explored the street culture of San Diego and Portland, but more so for the never-ending encouragement you gave me through this time.

Thank you to Elizabeth Mehren, my journalism mother, whose keen editing eyes and years of guidance were instrumental in bringing this book to fruition.

Thank you to my sister, Joy, and my brother-in-law, Alex, for supporting me through this process, whether it was offering up your dog for puppy therapy or providing wine. And I guess that means I should also thank Cinna, who is a very good boy indeed.

Thank you to my mother and father, who believed in me even when I did not. I grew up knowing love, a luxury so many kids I interviewed for this book were not afforded, and it was because of you two.

And to my husband, Drew: It is not lost on me that the longest amount of time we spent apart was in our first year of marriage, as I left you on your own repeatedly so I could report out this book. Through it all, you remained steadfast. I love you.

NOTES

Prologue: The Cabin in Oregon

Morrison Haze Lampley, interview by Vivian Ho, Marin County Jail, San Rafael, California, May 11, 2016.

Morrison Haze Lampley, interview by Vivian Ho, California Substance Abuse Treatment Facility, Corcoran, California, April 8, 2018.

Chapter One: San Rafael, California,

April 2017

Vivian Ho, "Victims' Families Cry as Killers Are Sentenced in Marin County," *San Francisco Chronicle*, April 18, 2017, https://www.sfgate.com/crime/article/drifters-to-be-sentenced-in-murderous-bay-area-11080637.php.

Morrison Haze Lampley, interview by Vivian Ho, California Substance Abuse Treatment Facility, Corcoran, California, April 15, 2018.

Vivian Ho, "Transients Plead Guilty in Slayings of SF Backpacker, Marin Hiker," *San Francisco Chronicle*, February 7, 2017, https://www.sfgate.com/crime/article/transients-plead-guilty-in-slayings-of-sf-10912830.php.

Vivian Ho, "Prosecutors: Trio Tied to Marin Slaying Used Blood-Moistened Cash," *San Francisco Chronicle*, September 23, 2016, https://www.sfgate.com/crime/article/prosecutors-drifters-in-marin-sf-slayings-used-9240790.php.

Jonah Owen Lamb, "Accused Murder Trio Reportedly Beat Man on Haight Street," *San Francisco Examiner*, October 22, 2015, http://www.sfexaminer.com/accused-murder-trio-reported-to-have-had-violent-past.

Gary Klien, "Three Murder Suspects Deny Guilt in San Francisco and Marin Shootings," *Marin Independent Journal*, November 20, 2015, https://www.marinij.com/2015/11/20/three-murder-suspects-deny-guilt-in-san-francisco-and-marin-shootings.

Kale Williams, Vivian Ho, and Kevin Fagan, "On S.F.'s Haight Street, Drifters Accused of Killings Put People On Edge," *San Francisco Chronicle*, October 14, 2015, https://www.sfgate.com/news/article/suspects-in-two-high-profile-bay-area-killings-6561227.php.

Federal Bureau of Investigation, "Uniform Crime Reporting (UCR) Program," https://ucr.fbi.gov/crime-in-the-u.s/2017/crime-in-the-u.s.-2017/topic-pages/expanded-homicide.

Vivian Ho, "As Distrust Grows in Haight, Street Kids Seek to Clean Up Image," *San Francisco Chronicle*, October 19, 2015, https://www.sfgate.com/crime/article/as-distrust-grows-in-haight-street-kids-seek-to-6575327.php.

M. H. Morton, A. Dworsky, and G. M. Samuels, *Missed Opportunities: Youth Homelessness in America; National Estimates* (Chicago: Chapin Hall at the University of Chicago, 2017), http://voicesofyouthcount. org/wp-content/uploads/2017/11/voyc-national-estimates-brief- chapin-hall-2017.pdf.

Christian Garmisa-Calinsky, interview by Vivian Ho, San Francisco, California, October 2015.

Chapter Two: San Francisco, California,

June 2011

Vivian Ho, "Buena Vista Park Neighbors Wary After Body Found," *San Francisco Chronicle*, June 18, 2011, https://www.sfgate.com/crime/ article/buena-vista-park-neighbors-wary-after-body-found-2367737. php.

David Thompson, interview by Vivian Ho, San Francisco, California, June 2011.

Bryan Samuels, interview by Vivian Ho, phone interview from Chicago, Illinois, December 8, 2017.

Michael Niman, interview by Vivian Ho, phone interview from Buffalo, New York, February 1, 2018.

M. H. Morton, A. Dworsky, and G. M. Samuels, *Missed Opportunities: Youth Homelessness in America; National Estimates* (Chicago: Chapin Hall at the University of Chicago, 2017), http://voicesofyouthcount.

org/wp-content/uploads/2017/11/voyc-national-estimates-brief-chapin-hall-2017.pdf.

Jamie Powlovich, interview by Vivian Ho, New York City, December 20, 2017.

Mindi Bowman, interview by Vivian Ho, Olympia, Washington, March 4, 2018.

Christian Garmisa-Calinsky, interview by Vivian Ho, San Francisco, California, October 2017.

Vivian Ho, "Harvey Milk Plaza: A Refuge for Transients," *San Francisco Chronicle*, September 26, 2012, https://www.sfgate.com/bayarea/article/harvey-milk-plaza-refuge-for-transients-3896752.php.

Vivian Ho, "SF Protester Sentenced for Throwing Bricks," *San Francisco Chronicle*, May 1, 2013, https://www.sfchronicle.com/crime/article/sf-protester-sentenced-for-throwing-bricks-4480915.php.

Vivian Ho, "Carjacking Suspect Shot at SFO Is IDd as Transient," *San Francisco Chronicle*, July 27, 2015, https://www.sfgate.com/crime/article/transiant-ided-as-airport-car-thief-shot-by-6408288.php.

Vivian Ho and Peter Fimrite, "Two More Suspects Held in Golden Gate Park Torture Slaying," *San Francisco Chronicle*, August 25, 2016, https://www.sfgate.com/crime/article/two-more-suspects-held-in-golden-gate-park-9182756.php.

Vivian Ho, "S.F. Street Kids Try to Oust 'Bad Elmo' at Wharf," *San Francisco Chronicle*, March 5, 2014, https://www.sfgate.com/crime/article/s-f-street-kids-try-to-oust-bad-elmo-at-wharf-5289295.php.

Chapter Three

Sleepy, interview by Vivian Ho, Tonto National Forest, Arizona, February 14, 2018.

Larry Beggs, *Huckleberry's for Runaways* (New York: Ballantine Books, 1969).

David Talbot, *Season of the Witch: Enchantment, Terror, and Deliverance in the City of Love* (New York: Free Press, 2013).

Patrick Lagacé, "Audrey, La Vie," *La Presse*, November 21, 2015, http://plus.lapresse.ca/screens/890bdef1-4446-4e4d-aa43-8764dca59d7c__7C___0.html.

Morrison Haze Lampley, interview by Vivian Ho, California Substance Abuse Treatment Facility, Corcoran, California, April 8, 2018.

Sean Angold's testimony, People of the State of California v. Morrison Haze Lampley, Sean Michael Angold, and Lila Scott Alligood (San Rafael, California, September 27, 2016).

Vivian Ho, "Druggie Drifters Said to Kill Rashly amid Dream of Starting Pot Farm," *San Francisco Chronicle*, September 27, 2016, https://www.sfgate.com/crime/article/druggie-drifters-said-to-kill-rashly-amid-dream-9298277.php.

Vivian Ho, "Details of Bay Area Drifter Killings Emerge in Marin County Hearing," *San Francisco Chronicle*, September 23, 2016, https://www.sfgate.com/crime/article/details-of-bay-area-drifter-killings-emerge-in-9235200.php.

Morrison Haze Lampley, interview by Vivian Ho, California Substance Abuse Treatment Facility, Corcoran, California, March 25, 2018.

Investigator who spoke on the condition of anonymity, phone interview by Vivian Ho, March 22, 2018.

Sean Angold, interview by Vivian Ho, phone interview from California State Prison, Corcoran, California, February 9, 2018.

Morrison Haze Lampley, interview by Vivian Ho, Marin County Jail, San Rafael, California, May 11, 2016.

Morrison Haze Lampley, interview by Vivian Ho, California Substance Abuse Treatment Facility, Corcoran, California, April 7, 2018.

Morrison Haze Lampley, interview by Vivian Ho, California Substance Abuse Treatment Facility, Corcoran, California, April 14, 2018.

Chapter Four

Morrison Haze Lampley, interview by Vivian Ho, California Substance Abuse Treatment Facility, Corcoran, California, March 25, 2018.

Mindi Bowman, interview by Vivian Ho, phone interview from Olympia, Washington, December 17, 2017.

Half brother of Morrison Haze Lampley who asked that his name not be used, interview by Vivian Ho, Facebook chat, March 26, 2018.

Grandmother of Morrison Haze Lampley who asked that her name not be used, email to Vivian Ho, November 16, 2018.

Morrison Haze Lampley, interview by Vivian Ho, California Substance Abuse Treatment Facility, Corcoran, California, March 24, 2018.

The National Child Traumatic Stress Network Complex Trauma Task Force, "Complex Trauma in Children and Adolescents," 2004, https://pdfs.semanticscholar.org/9f3a/08e62ddf4432bc9250f78de3043945318163.pdf.

Georgia M. Winters and Elizabeth L. Jeglic, "Stages of Sexual Grooming: Recognizing Potentially Predatory Behaviors of Child Molesters," in *Deviant Behavior* 38, no. 6 (September 2016): 724–733.

M. L. Hoffman, "Toward a Comprehensive Empathy-Based Theory of Prosocial Moral Development," in *Constructive and Destructive Behavior: Implications for Family, School, and Society*, ed. A. C. Bohart and D. J. Stipek (Washington, DC: American Psychological Association, 2001), 61–86.

Center for Sex Offender Management, "The Role of the Victim and Victim Advocate in Managing Sex Offenders: A Training Curriculum; Section 2: Understanding Sexual Assault from a Victim's Perspective; Topic: Intrafamilial Sexual Abuse," www.csom.org/train/victim/2/2_6.htm.

Chapter Five: Old Railroad Grade Fire Road,

Marin County, California

Sean Angold's testimony, People of the State of California v. Morrison Haze Lampley, Sean Michael Angold, and Lila Scott Alligood (San Rafael, California, September 27, 2016).

Morrison Haze Lampley, interview by Vivian Ho, California Substance Abuse Treatment Facility, Corcoran, California, March 24, 2018.

Lokita Carter, *I Am Not My Body* (blog), https://lokitacarter.com/blog.

Morrison Haze Lampley, interview by Vivian Ho, California Substance Abuse Treatment Facility, Corcoran, California, April 14, 2018.

Rob Sidon, "Tantra Teacher Lokita Carter's Triple Tragedy: Open Hearted in the Face of Cancer, Fire, and the Reckless Murder of Steve," *Common Ground*, February 2016, http://lokitacarter.com/wp-content/uploads/2016/02/lokita-common-ground-interview.pdf.

Chapter Six: Ocean Beach,

San Diego, California

Morrison Haze Lampley, interview by Vivian Ho, California Substance Abuse Treatment Facility, Corcoran, California, March 24, 2018.

Reddit.com, "Vagabond: A Digital Community Created by Vagabonds, for Vagabonds," https://www.reddit.com/r/vagabond.

Jonny Hurst, interview by Vivian Ho, San Diego, California, February 19, 2018.

Johnny Carrick, interview by Vivian Ho, San Diego, California, February 19, 2018.

Shay Ward, interview by Vivian Ho, San Diego, California, February 19, 2018.

Edie Ward, interview by Vivian Ho, San Diego, California, February 19, 2018.

Mindi Bowman, interview by Vivian Ho, phone interview from Olympia, Washington, December 17, 2017.

Morrison Haze Lampley, interview by Vivian Ho, California Substance Abuse Treatment Facility, Corcoran, California, March 25, 2018.

Chapter Seven: The Phases of the Moon

Morrison Haze Lampley, interview by Vivian Ho, California Substance Abuse Treatment Facility, Corcoran, California, April 8, 2018.

Morrison Haze Lampley, interview by Vivian Ho, California Substance Abuse Treatment Facility, Corcoran, California, March 25, 2018.

Investigator who spoke on the condition of anonymity, phone interview by Vivian Ho, March 22, 2018.

Facebook.com, "Māhealani Lila Alligood," https://www.facebook.com/lila.alligood.

Former friend of Lila Alligood who asked to be identified only as Kay, phone interview by Vivian Ho, September 10, 2018.

Morrison Haze Lampley, interview by Vivian Ho, Marin County Jail, San Rafael, California, May 11, 2016.

Chapter Eight: Haight Street,

San Francisco, California

Public neighborhood meeting in San Francisco, California, October 13, 2015.

Christian Garmisa-Calinsky, interview by Vivian Ho, San Francisco, California, October 2017.

Heather Knight, "Income Inequality On Par with Developing Nations," *San Francisco Chronicle*, June 25, 2014, https://www.sfgate.com/bayarea/article/income-inequality-on-par-with-developing-nations-5486434.php.

Wendy Lee, "Silicon Valley Bus Drivers Sleep in Parking Lots. They May Have to Make Way for Development," *San Francisco Chronicle*, June 25, 2018, https://www.sfchronicle.com/business/article/silicon-valley-bus-drivers-sleep-in-parking-lots-13021743.php.

Trisha Thadani, "Median Income Soars in the Bay Area, but Some Are Left Out," *San Francisco Chronicle*, September 14, 2017, https://www.sfgate.com/business/article/median-income-soars-in-bay-area-but-some-are-12196055.php.

United States Census Bureau, *Income and Poverty in the United States: 2017*, https://www.census.gov/content/dam/Census/library/publications/2018/demo/p60-263.pdf.

Heather Knight, "Expected SF Teacher Raises Aren't Enough to Stem Exodus from Costly City," *San Francisco Chronicle*, November 7,

2017, https://www.sfchronicle.com/news/article/expected-sf-teacher-raises-aren-t-enough-to-12336403.php.

Adam Brinklow, "San Francisco's Median House Price Climbs to $1.61 Million," *SF Curbed*, April 5, 2018, https://sf.curbed.com/2018/4/5/17201888/san-francisco-median-home-house-price-average-2018.

United States Census Bureau, "QuickFacts: San Francisco County, California," https://www.census.gov/quickfacts/sanfranciscocountycalifornia.

Applied Survey Research, *2017 San Francisco Homeless Count and Survey: Comprehensive Report*, http://hsh.sfgov.org/wp-content/uploads/2017/06/2017-sf-point-in-time-count-general-final-6.21.17.pdf.

Christian Garmisa-Calinsky, interview by Vivian Ho, San Francisco, California, October 2015.

Maggie May, interview by Vivian Ho, San Francisco, California, October 2015.

Gary McCoy, interview by Vivian Ho, San Francisco, California, December 8, 2017.

Chapter Nine: Santa Rosa, California,

December 2017

Facebook.com, "Haze O'riley," https://www.facebook.com/profile.php?id=100008833931465.

Momo, interview by Vivian Ho, Santa Rosa, California, December 11, 2017.

Alyssa, interview by Vivian Ho, San Francisco, California, July 3, 2018.

Miriam Montes, interview by Vivian Ho, Portland, Oregon, March 1, 2018.

Stephanie, interview by Vivian Ho, Portland, Oregon, March 1, 2018.

Ventura County Sheriff's Office, "News Story: Arrest of Sexual Predator," July 6, 2018, https://local.nixle.com/alert/6670102.

ABC12 News Team, "Man Charged with 'Sadistic Torture Relationship' with 13-Year-Old After Missing Kid Sweep," June 19, 2018, https://www.abc12.com/content/news/man-charged-with-sadistic-torture-relationship-with-13-year-old-after-missing-kid-sweep-485934351.html.

Melissa Hanson, "Four Defendants Deemed Dangerous After Police Said They Held 16-Year-Old Girl Hostage, Drugged and Assaulted Her," *MassLive*, January 5, 2018, https://www.masslive.com/news/worcester/index.ssf/2018/01/four_defendants_deemed_dangero.html.

Colette L. Auerswald, Jessica S. Lin, and Andrea Parriott, "Six-Year Mortality in a Street-Recruited Cohort of Homeless Youth in San Francisco, California." *PeerJ—The Journal of Life and Environmental Sciences*, April 14, 2016, https://peerj.com/articles/1909.

Morrison Haze Lampley, interview by Vivian Ho, California Substance Abuse Treatment Facility, Corcoran, California, March 25, 2018.

Chapter Ten: Under the Rainbow

Michael Niman, *People of the Rainbow: A Nomadic Utopia* (Knoxville: University of Tennessee Press, 1997).

Michael Niman, interview by Vivian Ho, phone interview from Buffalo, New York, February 1, 2018.

Adam Buxbaum, phone interview by Vivian Ho, December 8, 2017.

Nathan Akre, interview by Vivian Ho, Tonto National Forest, Arizona, February 14, 2018.

Snowflake, interview by Vivian Ho, Tonto National Forest, Arizona, February 13, 2018.

Adam Buxbaum, phone interview by Vivian Ho, March 1, 2018.

Sleepy, interview by Vivian Ho, Tonto National Forest, Arizona, February 14, 2018.

Momo, interview by Vivian Ho, Santa Rosa, California, December 11, 2017.

Morrison Haze Lampley, interview by Vivian Ho, California Substance Abuse Treatment Facility, Corcoran, California, April 15, 2018.

Mindi Bowman, interview by Vivian Ho, Olympia, Washington, March 4, 2018.

Sean Angold, interview by Vivian Ho, phone interview from California State Prison, Corcoran, California, February 9, 2018.

Chapter Eleven: Corcoran, California,

Spring 2018

Morrison Haze Lampley, interview by Vivian Ho, California Substance Abuse Treatment Facility, Corcoran, California, March 24, 2018.

Morrison Haze Lampley, interview by Vivian Ho, California Substance Abuse Treatment Facility, Corcoran, California, March 25, 2018.

Morrison Haze Lampley, interview by Vivian Ho, California Substance Abuse Treatment Facility, Corcoran, California, April 7, 2018.

Morrison Haze Lampley, interview by Vivian Ho, California Substance Abuse Treatment Facility, Corcoran, California, April 8, 2018.

Morrison Haze Lampley, interview by Vivian Ho, California Substance Abuse Treatment Facility, Corcoran, California, April 14, 2018.

Morrison Haze Lampley, interview by Vivian Ho, California Substance Abuse Treatment Facility, Corcoran, California, April 15, 2018.

Morrison Haze Lampley, interview by Vivian Ho, Marin County Jail, San Rafael, California, May 11, 2016.

Doug Styles, interview by Vivian Ho, San Francisco, California, January 11, 2018.

Chapter Twelve: Portland, Oregon

Morrison Haze Lampley, interview by Vivian Ho, California Substance Abuse Treatment Facility, Corcoran, California, April 14, 2018.

Denis Theriault, "Homeless Suspect in California Killing Drifted in and out of Portland," *The Oregonian*, October 8, 2015, https://www.oregonlive.com/portland/index.ssf/2015/10/homeless_suspect_in_california.html.

Evan Sernoffsky, "At Portland Soup Kitchen, Shock Over the Murder Arrests of 3 Drifters," *San Francisco Chronicle*, October 14, 2015, https://www.sfgate.com/crime/article/at-portland-soup-kitchen-shock-over-the-murder-6562439.php.

Miriam Montes, interview by Vivian Ho, Portland, Oregon, March 1, 2018.

Stephanie, interview by Vivian Ho, Portland, Oregon, March 1, 2018.

Chapter Thirteen: San Francisco, California, July 2018

Alyssa, interview by Vivian Ho, San Francisco, California, July 3, 2018.

Chapter Fourteen: The Road from Here

Vivian Ho, "Victims' Families Cry as Killers Are Sentenced in Marin County," *San Francisco Chronicle*, April 18, 2017, https://www.sfgate.com/crime/article/drifters-to-be-sentenced-in-murderous-bay-area-11080637.php.

Morrison Haze Lampley, interview by Vivian Ho, California Substance Abuse Treatment Facility, Corcoran, California, April 15, 2018.

Christian Garmisa-Calinsky, interview by Vivian Ho, San Francisco, California, October 2017.

Miriam Montes, interview by Vivian Ho, Portland, Oregon, March 1, 2018.

Momo, interview by Vivian Ho, Santa Rosa, California, December 11, 2017.

Gary McCoy, interview by Vivian Ho, San Francisco, California, December 8, 2017.

Michael Niman, interview by Vivian Ho, phone interview from Buffalo, New York, February 1, 2018.

Rick Misener, interview by Vivian Ho, Los Angeles, California, May 15, 2018.

Rob Allbee, interview by Vivian Ho, Sacramento, California, May 13, 2018.

Vivian Ho, "Outside Voices: Life After *The Work*," *Topic*, June 6, 2018, https://www.topic.com/outside-voices-life-after-the-work.

Miscellaneous Research

Brianna Karp, *The Girl's Guide to Homelessness: A Memoir* (Toronto, Canada: Harlequin, 2011).

Liz Murray, *Breaking Night: A Memoir of Forgiveness, Survival, and My Journey from Homeless to Harvard* (New York: Hachette Books, 2010).

Ted Conover, *Rolling Nowhere: Riding the Rails with America's Hoboes* (New York: Vintage Books, 2001).

Jeannette Walls, *The Glass Castle* (New York: Scribner, 2009).

ABOUT THE AUTHOR

Photo © 2019 Gabrielle Canon

Vivian Ho is an award-winning journalist who has written for the *San Francisco Chronicle*, the *Guardian*, *Topic*, and the *Boston Globe*. Raised in New England, she currently lives in San Francisco.